The Bonobo Gene

WHY MEN CAN BE SO DUMB

Steve Marshall

In memory of

Creighton King

whose creativity, wisdom and wit

really helped in the writing of this book.

"Men are stupid, and women are crazy.
Women are crazy ***because*** *men are stupid."*
- George Carlin

for

Sam & Jed

What people are saying about *The Bonobo Gene*

"I learnt a lot and laughed a lot.
Who knew one appendage could be so entertaining?"
Jane Kennedy, Working Dog

"I'm just glad I'm not in it."
Dermott Brereton, *Australian Football Legend*

"I have worked with Steve, and there is no-one who understands more deeply just how stupid men can be."
Titus O'Reily, *Writer & Comedian*

"A literary tour de force. I commend Steve and the eleven other chimpanzees that wrote it."
Trevor Marmalade, *Writer & Comedian*

"All hail The Bonobo Gene! An extremely humorous collection of stories about Stupid Male Behaviour."
Jennifer Hansen, *Journalist, Broadcaster*

"An uproariously funny, laugh out loud read. Steve definitely has the gene!"
Lawrence Mooney, *Writer & Comedian*

"I was a big fan of the TV show 'Men Behaving Badly.' Now we have the textbook."
Andrew Brooke, *Former CEO, Grundy Entertainment*

"Well done, Steve. Who knew there was a 'b' at the end of 'dumb'?"
Larry Emdur, *TV Host*

Published by:
Wilkinson Publishing Pty Ltd
ACN 006 042 173
PO Box 24135
Melbourne, Vic 3001
Ph: 03 9654 5446

enquiries@wilkinsonpublishing.com.au
www.wilkinsonpublishing.com.au

Copyright © 2023 Steve Marshall

All rights reserved. No part of this publication may be reproduced, stored in a retrieval system or transmitted in any form by any means without the prior permission of the copyright owner. Enquiries should be made to the publisher.

Every effort has been made to ensure that this book is free from error or omissions. However, the Publisher, the Author, the Editor or their respective employees or agents, shall not accept responsibility for injury, loss or damage occasioned to any person acting or refraining from action as a result of material in this book whether or not such injury, loss or damage is in any way due to any negligent act or omission, breach of duty or default on the part of the Publisher, the Author, the Editor, or their respective employees or agents.

Title: The Bonobo Gene. Why men can be so dumb.

ISBN: 9781922810717

A catalogue record of this book is available from the National Library of Australia.

Design by Spike Creative Pty Ltd
Ph: (03) 9427 9500
spikecreative.com.au
Printed and bound in Australia by Ligare Book Printers.

CONTENTS

A NOTE FROM THE AUTHOR

"It took me 10 years to live, and 2 years to write".

So said Bob Dylan about his classic song *"Tangled Up In Blue"*.

Only an idiot would dare compare themselves to Dylan, and I would never be that presumptuous, though I will say the gestation period of this slim tome has taken a couple of years to write after many decades of being a man, living with men, playing sport with men, and observing men.

So who am I? Started off as a radio copywriter, tried to be a TV publicist (no good at that!), then TV production, script writing, game shows, docos and comedy shows.

Some of the programs included *"Sale of the Century"*, *"The Price Is Right"*, *"The Eric Bana Show"* and *"Good Morning Australia"*.

A founding member of Triple M radio's Saturday morning juggernaut *"The Grill Team"* (under the idiotic pseudonym *"Sergio Paradise"*) then plenty more radio stations, and in recent years a hit podcast with the great Titus O'Reily. Titus and I even did a sold out seven-shows-in-seven-nights Australian tour (he as the headliner of course).

Born, raised and schooled in Melbourne, lived in the US for a while, ran a family toy company, and have now gone full circle by putting words on paper. But not on the dusty IBM Selectric typewriter I first used in the 80s.

Married with two teenage boys. The youngest barracks for Collingwood. We call him "adopted".

Speaking of Bob Dylan – some twenty years ago I saw him walking along Acland Street in St Kilda (with a couple of minders) before his gig that night at the Palais. Five metres ahead of Dylan on the footpath, a ratty looking busker was halfway through a tortured version of *"Blowin' In The Wind"* when he looked up to see the World's Greatest Songwriter ambling his way. A look of panic crossed the busker's face and he quickly segued into The Troggs "Wild Thing". Dylan saw the whole thing but his demeanour never changed. Just kept walkin' with that inscrutable Dylan face. Now that is cool.

In my journey weaving together tales that blend humour, humanity, and a touch of Bonobo-esque mischief, I couldn't help but be swept away by the myriad of hilarious anecdotes that emerged.

Each story, a rollicking testament to the quirks of both men and women and the companions they hold dear— It's a roll call of human experiences that paints a vivid picture of our shared journey through life.

I'd like to invite you share your stories and join that roll call.

Yes, you, dear reader, regardless of your gender, hold within you a trove of anecdotes that deserve the spotlight. In fact, my research has revealed that everyone possesses a wealth of stories centred on our wonderfully imperfect human behaviour. Stories that are not only amusing but often imbued with a unique wit that reflects the beautiful tapestry of our lives.

The pages of future volumes of The Bonobo Gene are waiting to be filled with stories from all perspectives - fathers, mothers, sisters, brothers, lovers, ex-lovers, friends, colleagues who share a laugh at the water cooler (in person or virtual) – everyone.

No tale is too mundane or too outlandish (as long as it stays on the right side of legality, of course). The sole criterion is that it brings forth the gift of laughter.

At journey's end (for this book, page 142), you'll find details of the Bonobo Gene website and my email address, ready to receive your stories, your laughter, and your unique perspectives.

I hope you enjoy the book. I look forward to hearing from you.

Steve Marshall

INTRODUCTION

Men. Blokes. Guys. Idiots.

We can be some, all or none of these things. Depends when you catch us. And what you catch us doing.

Are we *Merely Male?*

Bad behaviour. Offensive behaviour. Can most often be summed up as "stupid behaviour".

Why? Is there really a built in character trait particular to males that might explain, if not *excuse* a lot of this stupid and egregious behaviour?

And what are "men" these days? Well, that's a subject for a different book.

This book will look into the history of poor male behaviour, the reasons for it, look at whether it's on the rise, and maybe float a theory or two…

Most men will recognise themselves at some point.

And I hope women will look at their husbands, partners, sons, brothers and work mates, then laugh and say, "Look, that's you!!"

And given recent speculation on gender, its origin and importance, we raise the question, "in the future, will men even be *necessary? Is there a future for men?*"

One thing that seems to get missed these days in all that's said about gender and the sexes is that, very generally speaking there still appears to be a fair amount of attraction between men and women.

And let's be honest – while most men have a natural propensity for idiocy, the mere male can still reach astonishing levels of brilliance, be it in the arts, business or on the sporting field.

For every drunken buffoon spotted pissing on a fence, one can openly point to the classy genius of Roger Federer.

For every shifty politician or dodgy salesman, we can offer the dishevelled but brilliant young Australian blokes who created Atlassian.

Whether you like it or not, a lot of the time many women still like men, and the world continues to spin on its axis.

Boy meets girl. Woman meets man. They're not the trendy, much ballyhooed couplings so talked about today, but they still happen. Of course there are countless permutations between the sexes. Always have been, always will be.

While we examine some of the history and reasons behind Dumb Male Behaviour, let's hope some of the more extreme examples become less frequent and, yes, dumb.

A kind of Dick Détente, if you will.

And finally, no book about incomprehensible male behaviour would be complete without some kind of roll call of penile infamy.

Now I'm not for one moment suggesting that men as a group are *stupid.* That would be absurd. However, when you look at some of the evidence and behaviour of a lot of men, you do sometimes scratch your head.

I am going to put it down to a theory. It is a theory with very limited research, and is yet to be proven.

It's called ***The Bonobo Gene.***

– Steve Marshall

2023

CLEVER DICKS

Think back to where you were on January 9, 2007.

Doesn't sound that long ago, does it?

Apple supremo Steve Jobs was about to front the Macworld conference in San Francisco, California to unveil the latest technological device from his rapidly expanding company.

Jobs's performances at these massive *nerd fests* had become legendary in their own right. With a combination of ego, chutzpah, genuine techno whizzkiddery, and mixed with even more ego, Apple's "new product" announcements were a heady mix that nearly always generated massive publicity for the new devices themselves, as well as reinforcing the *"cult of Steve"*.

Anyone would think the two Steves – Jobs and Wozniak – had created everything Apple purely on their own. It was a brilliant piece of marketing. Suddenly it was cool to be a pencilhead or geek. It helped that Apple co-founder Steve Wozniak had apparently swapped his neck for a Medusa-like mass of curls. He looked like the sort of bloke if you asked him to dig a hole, would re*design* a shovel rather than lift one.

These nerds really were *changing the world.*

All the lights and music, sturm und drang, rock star charisma of their media launches just made Jobs and his Apple products cooler and cooler.

Back in 1984 it was the Macintosh home computer.

In 1998 it was the iMac.

In 2001, the iPod music player and storage system.

"A thousand songs *in your pocket!*"

Rumours in the tech world abound that in 2007, Steve Jobs is about to reveal his plans to enter (and thus, *dominate)* the booming mobile phone market.

A notoriously prickly boss at the best of times, Jobs is more nervous than usual on the day. He is anxious that the big screen hardware behind him on stage is working perfectly. And at the rehearsal, it wasn't.

After all, there's no point being the world's greatest technological dork if your "overhead projector" doesn't click on when it's supposed to. Before they open the doors to the general public, Jobs is fiddling with the remote like a grandfather trying to reconnect his Foxtel cable. (*"Tell me again, what does HDMI stand for?"*)

Somewhere backstage, a sweating Apple employee is nervously wondering what careers might be going right now at, say, Microsoft.

Ding! All of a sudden it's working, and Jobs relaxes. Clad in his usual baggy dad jeans, sneakers and black turtleneck, Jobs walks on stage with the swagger of a true rock star.

> *"This is a day I have been looking forward to for two-and-a-half years. Every once in a while, a revolutionary product comes along that changes everything.*
>
> *And Apple is very fortunate that it has been able to introduce a few of these into the world.*
>
> *Today we're introducing three revolutionary products.*
>
> *The first is a wide screen iPod with touch controls.*
>
> *The second is a revolutionary mobile phone."*

When he says the words "mobile phone", the crowd erupts like they're watching the Beatles at Shea Stadium.

> *"And the third is a breakthrough internet communications device.*
>
> *These are not three separate devices. This is one device.*
>
> *And we are calling it iPhone."*

The crowd reaction couldn't have been wilder had the long-deceased John Lennon himself walked out and sung *"Day Tripper"*.

After the hooting and the hollering faded down, Steve Jobs then went on to demonstrate all the features of the new iPhone, including things called "apps", (which you would get from an "app store"), plus emailing and texting from the device, and its built-in iTunes store and music storage system.

When he demonstrates how the user can use their *fingers* to interact with the built-in screen, thus making the objects on the screen appear *larger,* the crowd howls like they're at a Hillsong revival show.

And while there is no "laying of the hands", it would be fair to say Jobs has the audience right in the middle of his palm. There's only one thing he hasn't pointed out....

You can also use the built-in, 2-megapixel camera to take a picture of your DICK!

And send it to anyone in your address book!!

Steve Jobs was never reluctant to take personal credit for the brilliant inventions of his vast Apple team, and it might be pushing it to credit him with inventing the *Dick Pic.*

After all, both Samsung and Sharp had had cameras in their phones years before Apple, but like just about everything else in their vast technological armory, Apple made it *easy to use.*

And use it we did.

And we're still using it. In fact, just about everyone is using it.

Every day, tens, if not hundreds of million digital photographs are emailed across the ether. Websites, chat rooms, apps; there is even (and this comes as no surprise) an online counterculture completely devoted to genital photography.

The future is Now. And in most cases, it's a megapixel, colour-corrected, white balanced, fully edited, non pixelated, clearly filtered photo of someone's dong.

"There's no point being the world's greatest technological dork if your overhead projector doesn't click on when it's supposed to".

THE BONOBO

Given that they share almost 99% of our human DNA, it's easy to see why chimpanzees are our closest living relative, and it's true that we did share a number of common ancestors several million years ago. The resemblance doesn't end in a test tube; like us, chimps play, socialize, cultivate friendships and wage war.

They even laugh when tickled, or when watching reruns of *The Castle.*

However, if we really want to know why kids' TV entertainer Pee Wee Herman got arrested in a Florida adult cinema and thought a good way to get off a public indecency charge was by offering to do a free gig for the local sheriff's department, the answer may lie at the hairy feet of another primate, the *Bonobo.*

Once referred to as the Pygmy Chimpanzee (or as it should be known these days, the *special needs chimpanzee),* the bonobo is a small, critically endangered ape found only in a remote corner of the Democratic Republic of Congo in Africa. With leaner bodies than the common chimp and a propensity to walk upright, the bonobo is a unique creature whose society is as complex and social as that of humans. Bonobos demonstrate a wide array of feelings and emotions, including patience, empathy, compassion and altruism.

They are also filthier than a Kombi van full of cricketers on an end-of-season trip.

Everything in the bonobo world, despite it being predominantly run by the females of the species, revolves around sex and/or masturbation. You'd think with the women in charge there'd be a bit more decorum.

But no.

If a bonobo is happy, it will have sex or masturbate. If it is sad, it will have sex or masturbate. If it's angry or frightened, it will have sex or masturbate.

And it will even do the same if you give it a gift. This is, in my mind, its most human-like trait.

If a troop of bonobos discover a new food source, there will be a full on, all in sex orgy. I'm surprised the NRL doesn't have a team called the Northern Beaches Bonobos. Though unlike rugby league players, bonobos actually communicate verbally, with a large vocabulary of sounds, gestures, and indeed, words.

Though most chimpanzees are thought to be the only animals other than humans to have sex for *fun*, and not just procreation, the bonobo takes this to a whole new level.

Males will have sex with other males. Males will have sex with females, and every combination therein. Oral sex, deep kissing, polyamory, the bonobo does it all. And does it often.

But it's not all fun and games. Male bonobos can also be very violent, the difference being that their altercations will inevitably end up in sex. It's a bit like shaking hands at the end of a tennis match.

Scientists have increasingly looked to our DNA to help explain some of our actions and behaviours. In the early nineties they discovered a gene they believed may explain why some people are more prone to violence and aggression than others. Quickly named the "warrior gene", it regulates an enzyme that breaks down neurotransmitters in the brain including dopamine and serotonin.

Humans have various forms of the gene, which results in different levels of enzymatic activity. The study found that people with low levels of this activity were more prone to anger and violence.

The correlation was first noted in the study of a large Dutch family whose male members were extremely violent. One tried to kill his boss by running him over, two were arsonists, one a rapist, and another tried to kill a hospital warden with a pitchfork. Let it also be noted for the record that the pitchfork is your traditional weapon of choice among animated cartoon characters.

Though this Dutch family may have been unlikely candidates for *Family Feud,* they were an obvious good source of study into genetic predilections to violence.

If science has turned to DNA to help explain some levels of violence, then logic would suggest that some explanation for unusual sexual activity could also be found in our genes.

Could it be that, out of that 98.7% common DNA, males also share some genetic link to the bonobo?

At the Friends of Bonobos Sanctuary in the republic of Congo, its executive director, who goes by the single name of Ino, has an even more radical theory.

While looking after the more than 2,000 bonobos at the sanctuary, Ino has seen a lot of their more human-like behavior, including kissing, and walking upright.

Nearly all the animals there were rescued after losing their parents to poachers, so Ino and his team have managed to forge close bonds with a large number of juvenile bonobos.

Ino has floated the theory, which even he has admitted is "a big claim", that humans are in fact a direct descendant of the bonobo, and that people may have evolved from this small region in the Congo.

Most other scientists have dismissed his idea as fanciful, but he is sticking to his guns.

"I may not be taken seriously now", he says, "but within fifteen or twenty years, my claim may prove to be true."

There it is. The idea. The link to our deep and dank genetic pool.

WEINER BY NAME...

One of the clubhouse leaders of this *Bonobo Gene* theory is surely the unfortunately named former American politician, Anthony Weiner.

A now convicted sex offender, Weiner was a Democrat who represented New York's ninth congressional district for seven terms from 1999 until 2011. He never polled less than 60% of the popular vote in an election, and his political star seemed forever on the rise.

Enter the Bonobo Gene.

Despite the seemingly boundless gap between the left and right, American politics is overwhelmingly conservative in matters of sex, and in June 2011, Anthony Weiner fell on his proverbial sword after being caught sending a suggestive photo to a woman via Twitter.

To be fair, the photo may have been technically "inappropriate", but it certainly wasn't what would these days be described as a "Dick Pic".

The *New York Post,* a Murdoch-owned daily paper that loves nothing more than a lascivious love scandal *("If you don't want to be on Page Six, don't do it!")* even printed Weiner's suggestive texts that he'd exchanged with the ("unrequited", he said) object of his desire.

Although New York may be one of the more progressive states in the Union, sex scandals are usually enough to finish any politician's career. Weiner at first claimed his Twitter feed had been hacked, and what he had done was "not illegal". As everyone knows, in the court of public opinion, legality has very little to do with it, and a defiant Weiner stood up to say very firmly, "I will not be resigning."

As week later he appeared on local television and said once again for the record, "I am not going to resign".

Then of course, he resigned.

In 2013, Weiner sent a number of sexually explicit pictures to a

22-year-old woman. Not a huge surprise by this stage, but the best bit was the pseudonym he used for himself while sexting. Weiner called himself *"Carlo Danger"*; and believe it or not, the object of his desires called herself *"Sydney Leathers"*, which I actually thought was a Parramatta bikies' boutique.

In 2017, Weiner then pleaded guilty to a charge of transferring obscene material to a minor, and was sentenced to 21 months in jail. He was released after serving 15 months.

Once behind bars, the former congressman and unsuccessful New York City mayoral candidate's fall from grace was complete.

After his release from prison, Anthony Weiner got a job as CEO of a Brooklyn-based company that specialized in recycled glass table tops. One tries to not read too much into that.

But after just a year in the role, Weiner was made redundant, which was an appropriate summation of pretty much his entire adult life.

FANNY BY GASLIGHT

If you discount any half baked theories about a small primate from central Africa, and invoke the work of scientists, the number of reasons for male stupidity expands exponentially.

American author David Buss is an *"evolutionary psychologist"* at the University of Texas in Austin, primarily researching in human sex differences in mate selection.

As possibly the only person in this book actually *qualified* to give an opinion, it's worth looking at some of Professor Buss's most interesting experiments.

He has conducted a study that tries to uncover where peoples' priorities lie concerning levels of attraction in both short-term and long-term mating strategies.

Each person was asked to reveal either the *face* or the body of potential partners.

Professor Buss found that men who favoured a short-term mating strategy (i.e. a one night stand) revealed the woman's body portrait and those who were after a long-term strategy (i.e. a *relationship)* revealed the picture of the woman's face.

Kind of like an adult version of the kids' boardgame *"Guess Who"*.

Interestingly, he found that women didn't favour either portrait, but instead made sensible enquiries regarding the man's health, stamina and resources.

While this may seem to be reinforcing long held stereotypes, the professor does argue that there is often a long line of environmental and "evolutionary" factors that contribute more to men's bad behaviour. As he points out, not all men behave badly all the time. Background behavioural factors have a big influence, as do childhood environments, parents and peers.

An example of mens' bad behaviour is the increasingly common act known as "*gaslighting*".

Gaslighting is the action of tricking or controlling someone by making them believe things that aren't true. The abusive person gaslights to isolate their partner, undermine their confidence and make them easier to control.

Some of the phrases commonly used by the successful gaslighter might include:

- *"That never happened..."*
- *"You're crazy, and other people think that too.."*
- *"Do you really think I'd make that up..."*
- *"You know I'd never intentionally hurt you..."*

There is precious little to explain or justify this type of behaviour, or the blokes who do it.

In my day, they were simply called a *prick.*

TOXIC MASCULINITY

It's a term encompassing a whole range of poor male behaviour. But what does it actually mean?

While there doesn't seem to be one definition, there are countless examples.

Praising men who have multiple sexual partners while expressing disgust at women who do the same is top of my list. Rejecting roles traditionally regarded as "women's work" is another. Abusive and aggressive behaviour, including violence, whether it be physical or verbal, goes without saying. There are countless other examples that are recognized as "toxic masculinity", but, in my opinion, they can nearly all be summed up by another long-term catchphrase: *"Don't be a dickhead"*.

Male, female, or something in between; nobody likes to be treated like that. It's the old *"treat someone the way you would want to be treated."* It's not hard to recognize or define.

If we bring the bonobo into it, even though this little chimp shares 98.7% of our DNA, as I have said earlier, it's that other 1.3% that causes all the problems.

If a troupe of bonobos was performing in a circus, say (and I don't believe this has ever happened), they'd likely be kept under control by a bloke whose defining characteristics would include chewing tobacco, wearing a bandanna and carrying a large club (for discipline).

Not I'm suggesting that toxic masculinity can be eliminated through beatings and withholding food and privileges (violence begats violence, remember), but when you look at some blokes' behaviour towards women, a decent whack behind the ear would often seem to be the only real and acceptable solution.

Created by Dutch sociologist Deert Hofstede, *The Masculinity Index* describes the degree to which traditional masculine values like competitiveness and the accumulation of wealth are valued over female values like relationship building and quality of life.

Using these parameters, with a rating of 95,the world's most masculine country is (and this came as something of a surprise), *Japan*. The most feminine society, with a rating of 5, is Sweden.

Other "masculine" cultures are the USA, Germany, the United Kingdom, Mexico, Australia and Italy.

"Feminine" cultures include the Netherlands, Spain, Thailand, Korea, Portugal, the Middle East and parts of Africa.

Regarding the Middle East, it's difficult to reconcile some countries as being more "feminine". Given that in parts of Iran recently, a large number of schools have been attacked with poisonous gas to try to stop girls from getting an education. In 2023. Seriously.

According to Dr. Hofstede (his name still makes him sound like a character from *The Simpsons)*, some of the principal characteristics of a masculine culture include:

A low number of women in politics, with the ideal icon being the soldier/warrior or successful entrepeneur. Not surprisingly, conflicts are primarily resolved through aggression. This masculine society is driven by competition, achievement and success.

Characteristics of a feminine culture include:

A high number of women in politics, with conflicts resolved through negotiation; arts and healing are more important than manufacturing and business; and the ideal icon is someone who helps and nurtures the community.

Given these contrasts, how do we resolve those general differences between general dumb male behaviour and brutal toxic masculinity?

I would still argue that a clip across the ear is a good way to start.

As for those who would poison girls schools on religious grounds, this is why cruise missiles were invented.

"Bonobos are also filthier than a Kombi Van full of cricketers on an end-of-season trip".

THE STORY OF ADAM

According to one biblical narrative (and there are plenty to choose from), Adam and Eve were the world's first man and woman, catapulted by God into the Garden of Eden.

God allegedly created Adam first and then produced his female partner using a piece of Adam's rib.

Adam and Eve were allowed to consume whatever they wanted from their garden (remember, it's all vegetarian), but were not to eat from the Tree Of The Knowledge of Good and Evil, which seems like a lot of responsibility to be heaped upon one plant.

Making the whole thing sound more Disney than divine, a talking serpent convinces Eve to eat the fruit from the forbidden tree. If this had been a Disney animation, I'd like to think the serpent would have been voiced by Nick Cave.

Being a bloke, Adam grabs a piece of the forbidden fruit as well. God is upset with the pair of them, and uses his almighty powers to carry out an immediate punishment.

Adam is told he will live a life of hard labour followed by death; the woman will be subordinate to Adam; and the snake, well everybody will hate snakes.

There is talk that Adam and Eve both hid their nakedness using leaves from the forbidden tree but this story varies according to which scripture it comes from.

The whole thing is not to be taken literally of course, but we can all easily understand that this could be the first recorded time a man did something stupid to try and impress a woman, only to have it blow up in his face.

"Tiresius apparently spent several years as a woman without once ever changing his pronouns".

THIS IS THE DAWNING OF THE AGE OF TIRESIAS

Greek and Roman mythology is full of unusual characters and situations, with many strange links to sex and/or the penis.

One such character is Tiresias, who makes his appearance in many stories of ancient Greek literature.

Apparently, Tiresias was a renowned seer or soothsayer. This of course was centuries before the famed prophet Nostradamus, and also centuries before astrology columns appeared in some of the world's dodgiest mass market magazines.

I have a friend who worked for many years at one of Australia's biggest selling "women's mags", and one of her jobs was to write the weekly astrology column.

"Where do you get your material from?," I once asked her.

"Make it up."

"As outlandish a prediction as possible?"

"The stupider the better."

It was actually one of the most popular pages in the magazine.

So how did Teresias receive the "gift" of second sight?

Well this could have come from the pen of my friend at *"No Idea"*. As far as things seen in the back pages of magazines are concerned, this had about as much scientific credibility as *"Sea Monkeys"* or *"X-Ray Spex"*.

Apparently Tiresias saw two snakes mating, took exception to this act of public herpetic copulation and belted (*"smote?"*) the rooting snakes with his staff.

Now I don't even know how snakes have sex. I think it most closely resembles an Italian chef trying to entwine two lengths of live linguine, albeit with heads that deliver venom.

Anyway, after belting the snakes with his staff, Tiresias not only was suddenly able to see into the future, but apparently was turned into a – get this – "*woman*".

For a bloke who could supposedly predict the future, I bet he didn't see *that* coming.

Tiresias then reportedly spent several years as a woman, without ever trying to change his/her pronouns.

Nearly a thousand days down the track, our gender fluid soothsayer not only stretched credibility, but may well have tweaked his lower back when he came across yet *another* two snakes having sex in public.

Now Tiresias was nothing if not consistent, and so pulled out his trusty staff and attacked these writhing pythons, immediately turning himself *back into a man...*

All this toing and froing made Tiresias something of a celebrity among the Greek gods, to the point that goddess Hera asked Tiresias to adjudicate in an argument she'd been having with an extremely macho god named Zeus.

The argument itself was something you might hear comedian Bill Burr discussing on stage – it was "who enjoys sex more – men or women?" And given Tiresias' experience as both sexes, Hera thought he would make the ideal adjudicator.

As far as judging was concerned, it wasn't exactly "*Dancing With the Stars*", but after much deliberation goddess Hera thought that men enjoyed sex more than women, and Zeus did the blokey thing and immediately took the opposite tack.

Tiresias's answer didn't please Hera. He said that of all the pleasure gained from sex, 90% of it went to the woman and only 10% to the men. As they would say these days, "look at the ratios".

So bitter that she'd lost the argument, legend goes that Hera then struck Teresias blind; a disability he would be destined to suffer the rest of his life.

There is another version to this story though. As told by extremely well-read British actor and comedian Stephen Fry, Teresias was actually struck blind by the goddess Athena after he had glimpsed her naked. This is sometimes known as the *Lara Bingle Defence.*

THE ROMANS

Roman marketing slogan: "We conquer, we pillage, we'll build you a new village."

There's a longstanding myth that the ancient Romans built better roads and infrastructure than we do today. Actually there's some truth in that claim, as many ancient Roman-built roads are still standing today, although most would not survive the huge amount of modern traffic.

The Roman roadways were built over multiple levels, with side trenches and retaining walls. Although there is no evidence to suggest they were manned by blokes carrying "Slow Down" and "Stop" signs.

The fact is, phallic symbols were commonly found on all manner of Roman infrastructure, from roads to houses to buildings and bridges. In fact the very famous Hadrian's Wall contains no fewer than 57 ancient "dick pics" emblazoned across it.

The Roman military regarded the penis as a symbol of power, which crossed with a soldier's innate masculinity, made the phallic symbol common throughout the time, and it was the legionnaires themselves that helped spread these ancient "Dick Pics" across the Roman empire.

Even in Cordoba, Spain, which was conquered by the Romans in 206 BC, archaeologists uncovered a sculpted phallic carving more than half a metre in length.

The ancient Romans and Greeks were never far from magic and the supposed "supernatural" powers, both of which were attributed in some small way to the penis.

When the ancient city of Pompeii was destroyed by the eruption of Mt Vesuvius in 79 AD, many of its buildings were decorated with penis drawing and sculptures. An archaeological dig in the 18th century even uncovered a series of penis-shaped wind chimes.

In Great Britain in 2020, a 2,000 year old penis-shaped pendant made of silver was discovered by a woman with a metal detector. It was 1.2 inches long. The pendant, not the metal detector.

So it appears that R-rated graffiti and artwork has been around for thousands of years at least, but it got a real shot in the arm in the twentieth century with the invention of both the felt pen and the paint spray can.

There had been some rudimentary felt tip pens since about 1910, but the breakthrough came in 1962.

Masao Miura and Yukio Horie ran a business in Japan making art materials when they came up with the idea of the fibre tip pen, which was basically feeding an ink supply through a felt nib.

It was ideal for both drawing and fine art and was quickly taken up by designers in their home country. The fibre tip pen hit the United Kingdom and the USA some five years later.

The pen was an advanced version of the *Magic Marker*, created in the USA in 1953 by inventor Sidney Rosenthal.

His device was basically a tube of ink with a felt wick and it quickly became popular for lettering, posters and general graphic design.

In Australia, the brand name *Texta* has become synonymous with pretty much all felt tipped pens, both with permanent and washable inks.

By the late sixties and early seventies, juvenile young men (let's be honest, it's nearly always *young men*) had the perfect set of writing implements at their disposal whenever they had the urge to draw on walls, footpaths, anything really.

They had already mastered the aerosol spray can, which had been patented in 1927 by Norwegian engineer Eric Rotheim.

When it comes to quick and stupid graffiti subjects, the *penis* has always been one of the faves. Celebrated British graffiti artist *Banksy* has never stooped so low; his work is generally classy, whimsical and satirical.

Banksy's most celebrated work, *Love Is In The Bin* is a partially shredded version of his famous graffiti work, *Girl With Balloon.* It was recently sold by Sotheby's for an eye watering *$29.9 million.*

Of course, for every Banksy there has to be a *Wanksy.*

Wanksy is a bloke armed with a spray can and very little wit who has made something of a name for himself by drawing dicks across countless London walls and subways. Fair to say, he'd be lucky to get 29 bucks for his most recent mural.

Public graffiti is in most jurisdictions, a criminal offence though it would be fair to say, the world's jails aren't overly populated by buffoons whose weapon of choice was a felt tipped pen.

In 2017, Hollywood writer/director Tony Yacenda combined the stupidity of obscene graffiti with the ever popular "true crime" television genre when he made the award-winning Netflix satire, *"American Vandal".*

The sixteen episode series follows a couple of high school would be documentarians as they try to uncover the truth about a disturbing afternoon when twenty-seven teachers had their cars *"daubed with dicks".*

Naturally, there is a ready made suspect, a fifteen-year-old idiot by the name of Dylan Maxwell, whose penchant for penile graffiti seems to make him an early candidate for school expulsion anyway. The series follows the making of a documentary to uncover the truth about the incident, and while it's very funny, the show's real strength lies in its accurate depiction of a serious "true crime" mini-series, with A-grade Hollywood production values and the use of relatively unknown actors playing the roles of Californian high school teachers and students.

It's a bit like *"The Yorkshire Ripper"* meets *"American Pie"*, and is still currently showing on Netflix.

"We wanted to explore the ancient art of genital origami".

DICK TRICKS

Male creativity doesn't end, however, with the Dick Pic.

If you were to ask any Australian comedy nerd which production won the Outright Best Show at the 1998 Melbourne International Comedy Festival, chances are they wouldn't immediately recall *"Puppetry of the Penis"*.

Unlike most of the audience members who would instantly recall their fumbling attempts at recreating the "wristwatch" or "hamburger" the moment they left the theatre.

"Puppetry of the Penis" was the brainchild (if that's the right word) of former Peninsula Grammar graduate Simon Morley and his best mate, fellow puppeteer David "Friendy" Friend.

First proposed as a "high art" calendar, Puppetry soon became a live show where the two men performed a series of "dick tricks" which they cunningly described as "installations".

Or as Simon says, "We wanted to explore the ancient art of genital origami".

Championed by Australian radio stars Mick Molloy and Tony Martin, Puppetry quickly outgrew the Melbourne Comedy Festival, and embarked on an eight month Australian tour.

The tour covered more than 20,000 kilometres and was filmed by Mick Molloy for a documentary he named "Tackle Happy".

Creator Simon Morley is fairly matter of fact about the charm and success of his show.

"It's about putting male genitalia in its flaccid form on a screen three stories high, and just having a laugh. Women love it because if they did it at home they'd crush their partner's ego. I think it's very healthy!"

"The secret of the show's success is that there is absolutely NO sexual innuendo. Apart from the actual penis, the show is squeaky clean!

After the sellout Australian tour, the Olde Country beckoned, and the boys took their show to the 2000 Edinburgh International Fringe Festival where they promptly sold out again.

An eagle-eyed London theatre producer saw the show, and immediately recognized the potential of live on stage *"manhood manipulation"*. Pretty soon, *Puppetry of the Penis* was opening for a six month stint on London's famous West End. It even became the "cool" show to see by A-list celebrities, with the likes of Hugh Grant, Elton John, Bono and David Beckham learning a few new dick tricks. Supermodel Naomi Campbell was spotted at the show one night with an entourage of fellow female models.

Then, after successful tours of the United Kingdom, Ireland and Canada, Simon & Friendy took their capes and ever expanding penile repertoire to the Mecca of Live Theatre…Broadway in New York City! The show ran on the famous 42nd Street for two years, and culminated with the boys' appearance on the *"Tonight Show with Jay Leno"*. While they didn't perform any tricks on the notoriously conservative free-to-air American television, Simon summed up the show to an incredulous Jay Leno by simply describing it as *"a party trick taken way too far"*.

Today, a licensed version of the show runs 52 weeks a year in Las Vegas. Not bad for a bunch of dick tricks.

Or as Simon says, *"It's merely secret men's business set in the suitable Australian climate"*.

Many years ago, I played Australian football. Not at the professional level, as described in the Hall of Shame chapters later in this book, but at very much an amateur level. No multi-million dollar playing contracts in the "ammos"; in fact, the competition's actual slogan was *"for the love of the game"*.

The standard may not have been as high as the pros on the field, but in the locker rooms, levels of immaturity were on a par with anything in the Big League.

Showering en masse after training and games was not only common but expected. These days, players seem more prudish about getting their gear off in front of teammates. But thirty years ago, nudity was a common, if not entirely essential part of the footballing world.

And as we saw with the ancient Romans and Greeks, when you combine naked blokes and sport, voyeurism takes on a whole new level.

And so it was in our amateur football club.

Two players in particular were generally regarded as the "best hung" among the sixty-strong playing group, and it was a dubious honor both were happy to exploit.

In the showers, I mean.

One player (let's call him *"Doug"*) had developed a party trick he liked to call *"the helicopter"*, where he would grab the base of his penis and twirl it as fast as he could in a generally clockwise direction. With the addition of shampoo, the "soapy helicopter" became a locker room installation *par excellence.*

Doug's best mate (let's call him *"Stu"*) was equally well endowed, and took most of his inspiration from our *"puppetry"* mates as discussed earlier.

It was only going to be a matter of time until someone decided that a "measuring off" competition between the two was to occur.

After training one Thursday evening, none other than the senior coach announced that the matter of "size" should finally be determined.

"Stu, Doug….let's work this out once and for all", he said.

A three-legged stool was brought into the showering area from the bar.

Upon the seat, the coach had drawn four goal posts in black texta.

"Put your dicks through the big sticks", he said, "and we'll measure the longest..."

The club doctor quickly produced a tape measure, and to the howling laughter of dozens of his teammates, Doug was crowned the *"longest dick"* at the club.

Until.

"Hang on a sec," yelled the Under Nineteens coach, who also happened too be the Head of Physics at the very prestigious private school linked to this football club.

"The most accurate way to measure actual size is by liquid displacement.

Length through the mini goal posts is all well and good, but it doesn't take into account penile girth. Quick, someone grab a pot glass full of water!"

It was rapidly becoming obvious that every football club should have a physics teacher on its coaching staff.

Both players then took turns to dip their members in the glass of liquid. Spillage was minimal, and the displaced water was measured in a separate container with as much accuracy as could be mustered under the circumstances.

With much fanfare it was decided that Doug had won on length through the posts, but Stu had won on displacement.

A draw was the most fitting result.

"One day I went to the toilet and it just fell off."

THE MAN WITH A PENIS ON HIS ARM

"The worst thing was hugging my Nan at Christmas and poking her in the eye."

Whenever Malcolm Macdonald tallied up the win/loss ratio on his "life" ledger, fair to say it mostly came up negative.

The 46-year-old Englishman had become homeless after a relationship breakdown, and as he says, *"just took more and more drugs"*.

After performing some do-it-yourself surgery on a bodily abscess, Malcolm developed a severe blood infection.

"Penis turned black. One day I went to the toilet and it just fell off."

Now there's a sentence you don't hear often.

Doctors managed to save his member but had to regrow much of the tissue, and so grafted it to his arm, where, due to hospital delays and Covid it stayed (dangled) for six long years.

In a 2022 BBC doco ("dickumentary?"), Malcolm called his doctor and said, *"Can you imagine six years of your life with a penis on your arm? It's fucked. I'll cut it off soon. I've had enough. I want this penis off my arm please."*

"Twelve years ago I had a job, a nice partner, bringing money in, food on the table. Baby comes along. Then the relationship wasn't too good, and I ended up living on the streets. Friend of mine had a garage, set myself up with a bed, sofa and TV. Locked myself away in there, and just did drugs. Ease the pain."

Got a perineal abscess between my buttocks, and it kept coming back. I said I'm not having any more operations on my bum, I'll do it myself. So I got a needle and popped it.

The old fingers starting going black, the old toes going black."

Malcolm got to the doctors in time for them to save his life but his penis was gone for good.

"Basically, I had a stump. Just fell off. It was horrible."

His only hope was a procedure known as phalloplasty, where surgeons take skin from the arm and create a new penis, then surgically transplant it to the groin. But for that extended (sic) period of time, its location wasn't where it should eventually be.

Finally, after six years waiting, Malcolm's new penis was removed from his forearm and re-attached in its rightful place. "It was a nine hour operation", says Malcolm.

Nerves and blood vessels were taken from his arm and stitched together in the pubis region to establish a blood supply to the manufactured penis. Urologists worked with plastic surgeons to make sure Macdonald would have a functioning urethra – meaning he can now pass urine normally.

Medics even installed two hand pumps so Malcolm can give himself an erection. He was even able to insist on an extra two inches in length from his original member size.

"It's a designer dick with a little bit extra", he says with the hint of a smirk.

Having a full sized penis dangling from his right arm was not without its obvious challenges.

"I did burn it a couple of times while cooking. Though occasionally for a laugh, I'd tuck my darts under it when I was at the pub. You've gotta have a sense of humour about it."

SOMETIMES THEY'RE DISPOSABLE...

Ever read the esteemed journal *"Progress In Biophysics and Molecular Biology"*?

Didn't think so. Not many people have.

The journal is a peer-reviewed scientific treatise that began in 1950 and has been publishing new and interesting (sometimes bizarre) scientific theories ever since.

Not long ago, with the backing of more than thirty highly regarded scientists, the journal floated the theory that octopuses were actual alien beings from outer space.

Now this sounds more like something from a James Cameron movie script, but the paper suggests that several hundred million years ago, octopuses could have arrived on earth as *"an already coherent group of functioning genes within cryopreserved and matrix protected fertilized octopus eggs."*

To be fair, the paper also states:

"The genetic divergence of octopus from its ancestral coleoid subclass is very great...its large brain and sophisticated nervous system, its camera-like eyes, flexible bodies, instantaneous camouflage via the ability to switch colour and shape are just a few of the striking features that appear suddenly on the evolutionary scene."

So there you have it. Next time you're chomping down on a chargrilled octopus tentacle, understand you may well be consuming the descendant of a three hundred million year old alien creature. And there seems to be no current scientific paper to back up the theory that they taste better drenched in chilli and extra virgin olive oil.

The octopus is an eight-limbed, soft bodied cephalopod with multiple hearts and nine brains, which is possibly eight-and-a-half more than former US congressman Anthony Weiner.

Widely regarded as the most intelligent of all invertebrates, the octopus possesses the same number of neurons as a dog. Not all dogs though. You'd have more chance of teaching an octopus to sit than say, an afghan hound.

There are countless examples of the octopus's unique, problem solving abilities, from opening screw top jars, to navigating mazes, even counting cards in a Las Vegas casino. OK I may have made that last one up, but there is no doubt they are fascinatingly gifted creatures.

When it comes to reproduction, not surprisingly the octopus does things a little different to the norm. Because they lack external genitalia, most use a modified arm to pass sperm to the female. These modified arms vary in appearance between the species. Some resemble a syringe, others a spoon, and in the case of the North Atlantic octopus, a smallish toast rack.

Notoriously individual creatures, octopuses are not known for their sense of community. Large congregations of the animals are rare. Although a scientific study on the effect of "party drugs" on invertebrates found that when given large doses of ecstasy (MDMA), octopuses became increasingly sociable with each other. Though there was precious little evidence that this extended to them waving eight legs in the air while singing "*The Only Way Is Up*".

As far as external use of their genitalia, the most intriguing of all the octopus species surely has to be the argonaut, which as well as being the only cephalopod to secrete and live in its own shell, takes its mating ritual to a virtually unheard-of extreme.

Being up to ten sizes smaller than the female argonaut, the male develops its modified arm in a pouch under its eye, and when the time is right, expels it toward the waiting female. This throwing of one's genitals at a passing female would be a skill much desired by teenage boys, though unlike the argonaut octopus, would not ensure the continuation of the species.

This should be forever known as *The Detachable Dick.*

The detachable dick concept reached its ultimate conclusion one unforgettable night in the home of a nondescript former US Marine from Niagara Falls in upstate New York.

A former US cop once told me that when searching a database for potential subjects, *"always look twice at the guys with double-barrelled Christian names. Often the extra syllable tries to compensate for a lack of brains."*

He was spot on when it came to John Wayne Bobbitt.

In June 1993, John Wayne returned to the family home in Manassas, Virginia after a night drinking. His wife Lorena claims he then raped her and fell asleep. She then snuck out to the kitchen and grabbed an eight-inch carving knife, returned to the bedroom, lifted the sheet and cut off her comatose husband's penis.

To her credit, a single slash seemed to do the job, leaving the dick in reasonable shape. There is no evidence to suggest that it writhed on the bedroom floor like the decapitated head of a rattlesnake. Though given John Wayne's pedigree, it would have come as little surprise.

Lorena then grabbed her husband's severed penis and took off in the family car, though her driving suffered by trying to do *two things at once.* After a couple of miles or so, she tossed her hubby's dick out the car window where it landed in a vacant lot conveniently located next to a 7/11. I say "conveniently", since the attending cops were able to easily pack the detached dick into a milkshake container full of crushed ice.

By this stage, the former Marine had awoken to find his marital bed covered in blood. Finding the blood was easier than finding his dick, since it had recently made a late night trip to the 7/11, something John Wayne only did when he'd run out of Marlboros.

"Lord, I am now but half a man!" he may or may not have cried. I suspect his first reaction may have been slightly more colourful.

After a nine-and-a-half hour operation, surgeons at the local hospital were able to re-attach John Wayne's recently detached dick, much to the surprise of the local cops, his wife Lorena, and I suspect, John himself.

This is where the whole sordid story should have probably ended, perhaps with the likely postscript of a colourful divorce hearing.

But this was America, and where some men might see *"I lost my penis"*, John Wayne Bobbitt could only see *"I now have a great opportunity"*.

Not Lorena Bobbitt though. She was charged with assault, and after a lengthy trial, was found not guilty *"due to insanity"*.

John Wayne was charged with his wife's rape and also acquitted. To the best of my knowledge, no one has ever been found not guilty in an American court *"due to stupidity"*.

You'd think a D-grade telemovie would soon rear its ugly head, but John Wayne had more grandiose plans. After all, losing one's penis to a temporarily insane woman armed with a kitchen knife was in John's mind, less of a catastrophic injury and more of a chance to "go into business".

A year later, he appeared in two hardcore porn movies, *"John Wayne Bobbitt: Uncut"* and the more artistically ambitious *"Franken-penis"*.

Apparently no penises were hurt in the production of those movies. And no, you can't find them on Netflix.

Three years later, John Wayne Bobbitt was flown to Australia by executives of the Seven television network to appear as a "guest star" on a new tonight show hosted by an up and coming young comedian and actor, Eric Bana.

In a strange kind of coincidence, Bana was to make his own big screen debut a couple of years later in a biopic about a bloke who cut off his own ears with a razor blade.

The critically acclaimed movie *"Chopper"* was Eric's ticket to Hollywood, and his enormous international success has come on the back of his phenomenal acting talent, and not any mistimed amputations.

To place John Wayne Bobbitt in some context for Aussie TV audiences, a number of comedy sketches were written and filmed with him prior to the show going to air. Truth be told, I was a writer and segment producer on *"Eric Live"*.

In one of the sketches, we took John Wayne to a Japanese teppanyaki restaurant where he was asked to "react" to the sight of the chef's flashing knife blades quickly and brutally slicing up several sausages. Sure, it was a pretty lame joke, but much to the director's frustration, John Wayne didn't even *get it*, let alone laugh.

After the TV show went to air though, several of us were in Eric's dressing room enjoying a quiet drink, where a far more animated than he ever was on the show John Wayne Bobbitt suddenly announced to all within earshot, *"So would you like to see it???"*

Suddenly, staff members and producers who were regarding the just aired programme as *"not their finest hour"*, quickly raided Eric's bar fridge and yelled "Yeah, let's see the damn thing!" or words to that effect.

I can safely say with some confidence that the stitching scars were exactly as you might have imagined them; perfectly symmetrical, like black texta marks around a (very small) tree trunk.

In recent years, John Wayne Bobbitt has appeared on the *World Wrestling Federation,* formed an unsuccessful band (*"The Severed Parts"*), and even served a short stint in jail for robbery. He has had three failed marriages, and lives on his own in Las Vegas.

His ex-wife is now known as Lorena Gallo, and trust me here – she will hang up the phone if you ring her from Australia claiming to be from a radio station.

"Always look for the guys with a double-barrelled Christian name. Often the extra syllable tries to compensate for a lack of brains."

THE NATURAL WORLD

Among the squillions of different creatures that populate the earth, one must wonder who or what came up with the original blueprints. Given the sheer inconsistency and unpredictable variations in design, one can only assume that a committee was involved. And if run by the government, it would surely have come in over budget.

Forget the old and uncomfortable questions about God vs Science. Once when asked about the possibility of God actually existing, the great actor and writer Stephen Fry said, *"Bone cancer in children? What's that all about?"* And it's a fair point. It seems to me that believers in an omnipotent deity dread science the same way vampires fear daylight.

There are thousands of species, millions of subspecies, and hundreds of million different creatures on earth. And in the physiognomy of every living animal (including man), nothing seems to vary more in design than the penis.

From the blue whale down to the flea, they all have dicks of varying shapes, sizes and function.

The echidna, a native Australian marsupial, has four penises, but as far as I know, never uses them all at once unless performing at a hens' night.

The echidna is of course a spiny, egg-laying mammal closely resembling a hedgehog or spiny anteater, and it uses its four headed member during copulation, as one might expect. Although it is a part time operation.

When "on the job", half the echidna's penises close down (that's *two* heads out of action), and the other two get to work on the important job of fertilization.

Now the next time the echidna gets busy, the unused penises take over. It's a bit like a "twelve hours on, twelve hours off" work schedule.

Like most things in the natural world, there is a method to this type of madness. The female echidna's reproductive tract actually has two branches, thus ensuring a perfectly successful fit.

The scary thing about the echidna's four-pronged penile weaponry is that, like the rest of the animal's body, they're covered in firm, spiny quills. The female echidna is not harmed by these dick spikes, and scientists theorize that they may somehow aid in fertilization.

Seems to me that the female echidna, like many other females, always gets the rough end of the stick.

One of the most beloved members of the animal kingdom is the dolphin. Good looking and intelligent, the dolphin is the Brad Pitt of the ocean. They also have what is known as a *prehensile penis,* meaning it can swivel, grab and grope, much like a human

This raises the obvious, if intemperate question, can the dolphin…. you know, *please* itself? Nobody seems to know, but its obvious dexterity makes it well suited to navigate the female dolphin's complex and labyrinthine reproductive tract.

Sex for dolphins is is also not just for reproduction. Like the Bonobo, they are one of the few members of the animal world who copulate purely for pleasure. After all, there's no point being that attractive if you don't make the most of it. Here again, we must acknowledge the fine work of Brad Pitt.

The pleasure part though can be fleeting – most dolphin sex lasts less than ten seconds, but its recovery time is impressive, being able to ejaculate up to eight times an hour.

This is known in scientific circles as *The Teenage Boy.*

"They call him Flipper, Flipper…faster than lightning…"

Hello sailor! The Blue Whale is the world's largest living creature, and not surprisingly, has a dick to match. A blue whale's penis can be up to 3 metres in length and 30cm in diameter. And its testicles can weight up to 70kg *each!*

In Herman Melville's classic novel, *"Moby Dick"*, the author suggests that the skin of a sperm whale's penis could be used as a full length floor mat.

The Argentine Bluebird Duck is one of the very few male birds that actually has a penis. Most birds are – to put it bluntly – *dickless.*

But this little blue duck more than makes up for it.

The bird itself grows to about 41cm long, but its penis can extend to 43cm! Work that out. And it's shaped like a corkscrew!

The female Argentine Bluebird duck is often seen flying *away* from an eager male – can you blame it? – and scientists believe the penis could have evolved to that absurd length to make forced copulation easier. Of course, the female could well be flying away to *escape from it.*

There's also no truth to the rumour that the Argentine Bluebird duck's corkscrew shaped penis has now been replaced with the more convenient screw top.

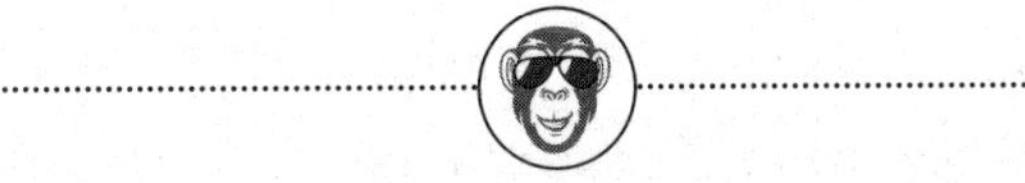

Another animal that is massively well endowed is the male sea turtle. With a body up to 2.5 metres long, the Softshell Leatherback turtle's penis can be half its body length. And at its business end lies a massive "head" that ejaculates from four out of its five lobes. It's a bit like the echidna. If the echidna had been designed by *"Alien"* director Ridley Scott

"The echidna has four penises but rarely uses them all at once, unless performing at a hen's night."

SO WHAT DOES PREHENSILE MEAN EXACTLY?

Only found in central America and parts of southeast Asia, the tapir is one of nature's most intriguing animals.

Large, forest dwelling mammals, they resemble a cross between a wild pig and an anteater, even though their closest relatives in the animal kingdom are horses and rhinos.

They can grow up to 300 kilos, and their prehensile snout can even be used like a *snorkel.*

We should acknowledge the word *"prehensile"* here. Basically it means "able to grasp things", as in monkeys have prehensile tails, thus allowing them to swing from tree to tree.

The tapir's prehensile nose lets the animal grab and rummage through leaves, fruit and other vegetation.

The tapir's most distinguishing feature though, is what earns it a mention in this book; its penis.

It too is a "prehensile" organ, with a gripping head on the end of its massive length. The tapir's penis can measure up to one third of its body length, and weigh as much as a single adult's leg.

The "gripping" part on the end is used to hold the female in place during sex. It has also been photographed using its penis to scratch its back. I am not making that up.

All hail the Tapir!

And finally, let's raise a glass to the much put upon Orb Spider. Given that 75% of the time, the female kills and eats the male after sex, the orb spider has an actual *detachable dick* that it places inside the female from a relatively safe distance.

Apparently, the weight saved by losing its penis in this way makes the orb spider stronger, thus making it less likely to be eaten by its mate.

EXPOSURE & THE ART OF EXHIBITIONISM

According to the *Encyclopaedia Britannica*, exhibitionism can be defined as *"deriving sexual gratification through a compulsive display of one's genitals."*

Note the word "compulsive".

The American Psychological Association even regards exhibitionism as a genuine psychiatric disorder, meaning that every time some bloke hits "send" on a dick pic, he could potentially wind up in the care of their very own Nurse Ratched.

With the proliferation of easy-to-use technology, is it any wonder men have so enthusiastically embraced the new art of electronic exhibitionism?

So have we *evolved* or *devolved* to the Dick Pic?

While it's safe to say we are living in a golden age of penile portraiture, male exhibitionism has a long and colourful history.

The Olympic Games began in southern Greece in 776 BC as a religious festival honouring the Greek god, Zeus.

Early Olympic events included athletic contests as well as chariot racing, wrestling and a number of combat sports.

Half a century later, a Spartan runner named Aganthus accidentally lost his loincloth mid race, thus ushering in a new era of nude competition. Not surprisingly, the naked competitors proved remarkably popular with both spectators and commentators alike. Although I'm not sure there were commentators in those days, as BC can also stand for "*before cameras*".

But to paraphrase an old joke about nude dancing, not everything stopped moving once one had crossed the finish line. At least it provided

Aganthus with somewhere to hang his gold medal. Or olive wreath, which is what the winners received in those days.

While the ancient Greeks often regarded nudity as a reflection of their gods, the Romans took a more prudish view, and tended to regard public nakedness as something to be avoided. Rugby League had not yet hit the Mediterranean.

That's not to say the nude wasn't well represented in a lot of ancient art.

To the Greeks, the ideal of masculine excellence was best expressed by the nude male body, though it's obvious when you study many ancient Greek statues that, in those days, size really *did* matter. And not in the way you might think. Back then, *smaller* was better. In fact, an overly large penis was regarded as somewhat uncouth.

So while the larger than life marble statues were often muscle bound, yes, *"Greek gods"*, most of them were demonstrably underhung.

These days, genital shrinkage is often linked to excessive use of anabolic steroids, especially in bodybuilders and athletes.

Finasteride, a hair loss medication once prescribed to British soccer star Wayne Rooney, is also known to cause genital shrinkage in some men. I'm not sure whether Rooney suffered any of these unfortunate side effects, but he does seem to have retained most of his hair, though this could be more due to a $15,000 transplant he had in 2011.

So if we accept that exhibitionism is a type of sexual fetish, where does it rate on the fetish ladder of shame?

Some would say that no fetish, as long as it's consensual and harmless, is shameful, but in my opinion, taking a digital picture of one's junk and posting it on the internet is rarely less than stupid.

So why do so many men like to send dick pics? It all seems fairly straight forward until you get the scientists involved. But before jumping to that level, best to ask blokes themselves.

I don't want to go out on too much of a limb here but I will suggest that as a general rule, *"I thought she'd like it"* is not always going to pass the pub test.

A recent American study on the subject concluded the main reason men send unsolicited dick pics is that of "transaction"; a 21st century version of the old "I'll show you mine if you show me yours" routine. While this might appear pretty obvious, it defies a common perception that the whole thing stems from a type of misogyny where men send the pic to express their hostility towards women.

I know a bloke who is something of a "Tinder head"; he trawls the online dating app religiously, hoping to hook up, or at least flirt with women who are inevitably far younger and more attractive than himself.

I asked him if he sent many unsolicited dick pics after an initial interaction with women on Tinder.

He looked at me as if I was mad.

"Of course I do. Jesus. That's why it was invented!"

Without reflecting too much on the Tinder inventor's intentions, I then asked him if he ever received something similar in return.

"Oh, about 20% of the time", he replied. This mainly told me there was a 75% chance he was lying.

But according to a study by *Cosmopolitan* magazine (yes, it still exists apparently), one of the reasons men send dick pics is to boost their low self esteem. How *this* works I have no idea.

But another recent, more scientific study also suggested that sending dick pics was indicative of a heightened level of narcissism, which surely makes more sense.

Either way, remember, before hitting *"send"*, double check the recipient is *"girl I met at sports bar"* and not *"mum"*.

MISSING THE POINT

After getting a sympathetic hearing from VICE Media reporter Alice Hines in a story about the difficulties convicted sex offenders have when re-entering society, a prisoner expressed his appreciation by sending Alice a Dick Pic.

STREAKING

Being a university student in Australia was never as much fun as anything dreamt up by US college magazine National Lampoon, and it must be said one of American college life's stupidest pastimes never really took off Down Under. And I don't mean fraternities and toga parties.

I speak of course, of *streaking.*

It may well be apocryphal, but the story goes that in 1974, a bunch of bored students at Florida State University decided to get naked and jog from one end of the campus to the other. No iPhones handy in 1974, but word spread quickly, and pretty soon, naked group jogging (or *streaking,* as it soon became known) was suddenly a hot activity at schools across the nation.

In the early eighties, I met a kid from Connecticut whose father had sent him to Australia after his final year of high school to work in the family business, before beginning college.

"If you're ever in Tuscaloosa, Alabama, you'll have to come visit", said Noel. A year or so later and I was embarked on my long dreamt about "road trip across America", and thus took a detour from New Orleans into the heart of Crimson Tide country. There began a hilarious three months at the famous University of Alabama.

Noel kindly invited me to sleep on a pullout mattress on the floor of his dorm room. There was one condition; I had to write all his English essays. *"You're a better writer than me,"* he said, an assertion backed by no evidence whatsoever.

Tuscaloosa might have been a big college town, but there was precious little public nudity. Definitely no streaking, although at the Friday night pep rallies before a big Crimson Tide football game, there'd be the occasional raising of a red top and exposure of a pair of breasts.

You always got the feeling that sprinting naked down Frat Row at the U of A would incur the wrath of the campus police, who all looked like William Shatner in *"T.J.Hooker"*.

Heavyset Southern cops with more spare fat than a George Foreman Grill.

Country music star Ray Stevens had a number one hit with the novelty song, *"The Streak"*. Now this should have been the moment when the whole stupid thing *"jumped the shark"*, as they say. But pretty soon, streaking became a solo activity. Combine that with professional sports, and streaking rapidly became the singular inane act that perfectly summed up the late seventies and early eighties.

In the same year the Florida State Seminoles got their gear off, Australian Michael O'Brien took streaking to the next level by running onto the field during an England-France rugby Test at Twickenham. O'Brien achieved some notoriety when local policeman Bruce Perry preserved the Aussie stockbroker's modesty with his well place police helmet, a move the cop deemed unnecessary.

"He didn't have much to cover up, to be honest".

In 1977, a frustrated Australian cricket captain Greg Chappell was so fed up with a streaker during a Test match against New Zealand that he whacked him across the arse with his bat, a move that unfortunately didn't end up as part of the Gray Nicholls company's marketing plans.

One of the most famous Australian sports streaks occurred in 1982 at the AFL Grand Final between Carlton and Richmond at the mighty Melbourne Cricket Ground.

In front of more than 107,000 spectators, a 17-year-old stripper from Adelaide's Crazy Horse Club by the name of Helen D'Amico took off across the hallowed turf clad only in a Carlton scarf.

As Tigers legend Kevin Bartlett said afterward, *"She was either blonde or dark, depending where you looked."*

Helen first made a beeline for Carlton backman Bruce Doull and his opponent, Richmond champ Jimmy Jess.

The notoriously reclusive Doull was quick to evade the naked young woman, until his teammate Wayne Johnston grabbed the end of her scarf and flung her to the ground.

D'Amico was fined $1,000 after the incident, and kept a relatively low profile until tracked down by the media in 2008. Now a grandmother, she simply described the event as *"an out of body experience. I was 17, I was stupid."*

Streaking at sports events is a rare occurrence these days, and anyone who got the urge to strip off and run across a sporting field would most likely face a huge fine and lifetime ban. Laws vary in different countries and jurisdictions and will generally cost you up to $5,000 to get your gear off and sprint across a playing field. And these days the security guards are pretty unforgiving also.

These days, running onto the hallowed turf of the Melbourne Cricket Ground (clothed or unclothed) will cost you in excess of A$11,300.

In the South Eastern Conference of American college sport, streaking fines start at $50,000 for a first offence, going up to $250,000 for a third offence. Though I'd suggest if you're able to dodge a massive college football defensive line more than twice while completely naked, you probably deserve to *win* $250,000.

"She was either blonde or dark,
depending where you looked."

DUMB DICKS PART 1

The Hall of Shame

According to Greek mythology, Narcissus was a young man inordinately impressed with his own good looks.

Sound familiar? Apparently he was admiring his reflection in a lake, and when trying to hug himself, toppled into the water and drowned.

This of course is where the word *narcissism* comes from, generally meaning a supreme level of arrogance or self regard. Or as we might say in Australia, "they're up themselves".

Not surprisingly, an absurdly high level of self regard is common among elite sportspeople, especially *men.*

Individual sportsmen, like tennis players and golfers, seem to possess massive levels of egocentricity, though both sports seem to have a relatively low number of poorly behaved individuals.

Whether it's the "mob mentality", or simple safety in numbers, it seems the largest number of idiot blokes come from within team sports.

In Australia, the two most popular team sports are Australian Rules football (*Australian Football League/AFL* and rugby league *(National Rugby League/NRL).*

One could make the argument that NRL sex scandals have exploded in number in recent years, but a more accurate take would be that the "broken nose brigade" have simply maintained a premiership-winning level of consistency as far as sex scandals go.

Either way, the Australian public now regards most of the NRL as having the collective IQ of firewood. And the AFL isn't much better.

Let's look at a few of the NRL's more notorious scandals in recent years...

Exhibit A: Mitchell Pearce

While playing for the Sydney Roosters in 2016, Pearce received the heaviest fine ever imposed on an Australian rugby league player when he was docked $125,000 and suspended for eight matches for simulating a sex act with a dog. One shudders to think of his penalty if the charges hadn't included the word *"simulated"*.

There was also no evidence to suggest that the act was "non-consensual". *"There's a good boy..."*

Pearce's canine tryst also occurred on ANZAC Day, possibly the holiest of dates on the Australian calendar.

One could naturally assume that the slew of bad publicity from such an act could possibly be career ending, But Mitchell Pearce was able to take some comfort from the fact that he was also Australia's Most Googled Man in all of 2016.

Pearce was then traded to arch rivals, the Newcastle Knights, where he was forced to call off his upcoming wedding to a former professional dancer after it was revealed he sent "flirty" text messages to a female member of the Knights staff. At the time, he was also club captain.

While none of his teammates have ever described him as anything but a "ripper bloke", if you were a contestant on *Who Wants To Be A Millionaire* and needed a quick answer to a tricky general knowledge question, you probably wouldn't choose Mitchell Pearce as your "phone-a-friend".

When the wedding text message story broke, Pearce quit the Knights and moved across the world to French club, the Catalan Dragons. Speaking about his aborted wedding plans, Pearce simply described the time as *"the worst year of my life"*.

There may well be a dog in Newcastle who would argue that point.....

Exhibit B: Tyrone May

Former Penrith Panther Tyrone May narrowly avoided jail time for producing sex tapes without the consent of the women involved. May made four tapes, including two videos shot during an orgy with teammates. After pleading guilty, the Samoan international received 300 hours of community service.

"Telling my family was the hardest thing", May told journalists afterward.

"I didn't realize how much drama and trouble I could cause. Once it's on the internet, it doesn't go away".

Correct, Tyrone. Have a pick of the board.

In 2018, a woman May had met on Facebook hooked up with the five eighth and another man at a hotel where the offence allegedly took place. Informed that several videos of the encounter had been distributed online, the woman contacted police and May was arrested.

Now playing for the aforementioned Catalan Dragons, who obviously have a "forgive and forget" attitude to player signings, May said during his courtroom ordeal, "If I was the father of a girl and that happened to her, I'd be pretty filthy, so I'm honestly sorry".

Exhibit C: Todd Carney

One of the NRL's finest players of recent times, Todd Carney won the prestigious Dally M medal playing for the Sydney Roosters in 2010. Carney also represented New South Wales in the State of Origin competition, and played a Test match for Australia in the same year.

It should be noted that Carney was let go by the Roosters for drink driving.

But it was an infamous photograph that surfaced in 2014 while playing for the Cronulla Sharks that enshrined Carney in Idiot Immortality.

The snap showed him urinating in his own mouth, a practice known as "*bubbling*".

Admittedly it's not a particularly well known or popular practice, and I think it's rare for blokes to be photographed while doing it.

Nonetheless, the Sharks were less than impressed, and sacked him immediately. Cronulla issued a statement saying the incident *"did not meet the values and standards the club is looking to uphold and take into the future."*

After destroying his NRL career, Carney moved to Europe where he played for – you guessed it – the Catalan Dragons.

Eight years later, an extremely contrite Todd Carney said, *"It's about knowing your limits, and who you are"*.

While "bubbling" may not be a hanging offence, it's definitely Group 1 standard in the "stupid stakes". And if nothing else, Carney should have a spot in the *"Dick Tricks Hall of Fame"*.

Exhibit D: John Hopoate

A powerfully built and sublimely talented junior athlete, Tongan-born John Hopoate joined the Manly-Warringah Sea Eagles in 1993 and seemed set for a long and successful career.

He played State of Origin in 1995, and was selected for the Tongan national rugby league team, although ended up representing Australia instead due to the residency rule.

After transferring to the newly merged West Tigers in 2000, Hopoate was suspended several times, including one game against the Melbourne Storm where he was cited for ten different violent incidents.

But it was in 2001 that John Hopoate outdid himself in the bad behaviour stakes. Early in a game against the North Queensland Cowboys, Hopoate inserted his middle finger into the anuses of three of his opponents. As one wit at the time said, "At least it was *during play*".

Hopoate was suspended for 12 matches, despite claiming he was just giving the players *"a wedgie"*.

But as Cowboys player Peter Jones said, *"I think I know the difference between a wedgie and having a finger stuck up my arse"*.

The remainder of Hopoate's NRL career was marred by controversy, and he retired from the Manly club in 2005 as

"the most suspended player of the modern era."

Hopoate then took up boxing, and held the Australian heavyweight championship from 2008-9. More fights occurred in and out of the ring, and he finally hung up the gloves after an unsuccessful fight against Cronulla strongman Paul Gallen in 2019.

Like many others unfortunately, Hopper was a gifted sportsman but a flawed talent. As he recognises, for the rest of his life, he will be known as the *"finger in the arse"* guy.

Now that's something a Bonobo *would* do.

DUMB DICKS PART 2

AFL SCANDALS

Exhibit A: WAYNE CAREY

Wayne "The Duck" Carey is widely regarded as one of, if not *the* greatest player to ever pull on an AFL guernsey. A powerfully built centre half forward, Carey could win games off his own boot, and helped carry an already powerful North Melbourne team to the 1996 and 1999 premierships.

A seven time All-Australian, Carey's life changed irrevocably in 2002 when, a mere twelve months after marrying his long term partner, he was caught in a "compromising position" with the wife of his premiership teammate and best friend, Anthony Stevens.

His downfall was swift. Carey tearfully resigned from the Kangaroos and was promptly signed by the Adelaide Crows where he lasted two seasons before retiring because of injury.

Since the infamous affair that according to former North Melbourne champion Brent Harvey *"set the club back five years"*, Carey's woes have included domestic violence charges and assault convictions. He has described the affair as *'the biggest regret of my life. It has haunted me for twenty years."*

In recent times, Carey has worked as a TV and radio commentator, but had to relinquish those roles in 2022 when he was caught with a small plastic bag of white powder at Crown Casino in Perth. No charges were laid after the incident, with Carey insisting the powder was merely *"crushed up anti inflammatories."*

Exhibit B: Ricky Nixon

By his own admission, Ricky Nixon was no superstar on the AFL field, but when his 63-game football career ended in 1993, he become one of the most influential off the field men in the game.

A year after his retirement, Nixon created his own player management agency, which immediately helped revolutionize how players and coaches were marketed and remunerated.

At its peak, Ricky's Flying Start company had on their books the absolute cream of the AFL talent pool, including such superstars as Gary Ablett Snr, Tony Lockett, Jason Dunstall, James Hird, and – here you go – Wayne Carey.

When he cleverly outsmarted the AFL salary cap in 2000 to gain Carey an extra $400,000 per year, Nixon reportedly told an unhappy CEO of the AFL, *"I run the competition, not you"*.

It's no exaggeration to say that today's fat football pay packets owe a great debt to Ricky Nixon's innovative and forward thinking business acumen a couple of decades ago.

But he wouldn't be in this book if somehow, The Dick hadn't, if you'll excuse the expression, *reared its ugly head.*

Ricky Nixon's downfall began in 2008 when he got involved with drugs, principally cocaine.

"I had never done drugs in my life", he said, *"and I got addicted"*.

Success often breeds hubris, and in my opinion, Ricky Nixon is the perfect example.

A couple of years later, Ricky was embroiled in what became known as the *"St Kilda schoolgirl"* scandal.

A 17-year-old student from a prominent girls' school had apparently become involved with a number of St Kilda footballers, and had then been photographed in a hotel bed with Ricky Nixon.

Nixon lost his accreditation with the AFL Players Association and ended up selling his Flying Start agency.

Trouble has since followed him, with various charges and controversies (mostly fairly minor, it must be said) having dogged his steps for years.

It was a sad fall from grace for the guy once described as

"the most powerful man in football."

Despite a couple of other minor legal issues, Ricky admirably seems to spend much of his time these days raising much needed money for struggling country and local football clubs.

Exhibit C: AFL execs caught with their pants down

Most footballing scandals involve players and former players. Rarely does the rank whiff of male stupidity permeate the walls of the all-powerful ruling body itself.

But that's what happened in 2021, when not one, but two high falutin' AFL executives were forced to resign after it was discovered they'd been sleeping with junior female staff members.

Football Operations Manager Simon Lethlean and commercial General Manager Richard Simpkiss both fell on their proverbial swords for having, in the words of AFL CEO Gillon McLachlan, *"inappropriate relationships"*.

McLachlan went on to say, *"I expect my executives to be role models, and should set a standard of behaviour for the rest of the organisation. They are judged, as they should be, to a higher standard."*

You may have expected the pair to lay low for a while (or at least join the Catalan Dragons), but in the usual way of the AFL boys' club, once you're part of the inner sanctum, transgressions are quickly glossed over and forgotten.

Before you could say "jobs for the boys", Lethlean had been quickly installed as Football Manager at the St Kilda Football Club, and took over as the club's CEO at the end of the 2022 season.

He quickly made his presence felt in late 2022 by being part of the group who sacked senior coach, Brett Ratten.

Richard Simpkiss didn't rest on his laurels either. Within months he had been hired by Croc Media chief Craig Hutchison to join the radio conglomerate's commercial department.

Perhaps in the AFL, if you're going to be an idiot, best you wear a suit rather than a jumper.

BATTLE OF THE SEXES

The description has been used to describe everything from ongoing social phenomena to cheap and tacky TV game shows.

Funnily enough, if you Google the phrase, the first thing to come up is tennis legend Billie Jean King's 1973 match against Bobby Riggs. A former highly ranked tennis pro, Riggs was also a hustler and promo specialist, and had beaten Australian star Margaret Court in straight sets some months earlier; a match that became known as the *"Mother's Day Massacre"*.

The $100,000 winner takes all purse helped the much hyped event reach a staggering number of spectators, with the world TV audience estimated at around 100 million.

Bobby Riggs, a pepped up shyster of the highest order, played the sexist card throughout the lead up, and it was soon hyped into something of a grudge match. He even entered the court in a rickshaw surrounded by statuesque women and wearing a warm up jacket with the words "Sugar Daddy" emblazoned across the back.

As it turned out, Billie Jean and Riggs ended up as life long friends, and she spoke to him the day before he died of prostate cancer in 1995.

A movie about the famous match, starring Emma Stone and Steve Carell was released via Netflix in 2017. It received generally favourable reviews, despite some of its slightly dodgy on court tennis scenes.

These intersex tennis matches seem very much a 1970's thing, though the format was renewed in 1992 when American legend Jimmy Connors took on 18-time Grand Slam winner Martina Navratilova at Caesar's Palace in Las Vegas.

Connors, the two-time Wimbledon champ reclaimed a little pride for mere males when he defeated Martina in straight sets, 7-5, 6-2. Each player received $500,000 with an extra half a million for the winner. Connors also revealed a decade later that he had place a $1 million bet on himself to win in straight sets. *"It's good to be the unofficial women's champion now"*, he said after the match.

It's hard to imagine a similar match happening these days – Novak Djokovic vs Serena Williams would be a promoter's dream on paper, but it would never happen.

In the late 1990's, there was an Australian TV game show named *"Battle of the Sexes"*, which enjoyed a couple of seasons on air, though it never rated particularly highly.

Based on a popular radio quiz segment, the show was hosted by commercial DJ Ed Phillips, and featured teams from both sexes battling it out over a series of questions about their opposite number. The losing team had to then perform a zany stunt to be broadcast at a future date.

The show never really caught on in a big way despite its theme music being "Macho Man" by the Village People, and it's perhaps telling that over the course of its 95 episodes, the Women's teams defeated the Men's teams quite comfortably. As its former producer told me, *"The one thing to come out of Battle of the Sexes is that it was obvious that women knew a lot more about men than men knew about women"*.

For those like myself, who believe in the Bonobo Gene theory, this observation will come as no great surprise.

In 1983, Australia's Network Ten struck gold when it needed to provide a higher rating lead in program to its 6pm news hour. Enter the Grundy-produced *"Perfect Match"*, hosted by radio DJ Greg Evans and blonde model Tiffany Lamb.

The premise was game show simplicity. A single asks questions of three unseen (opposite sex) singles then picks one to go on a date. The game is then reversed along sex lines. The difference was that most of the "dates" were accompanied by a film crew, who would hopefully unearth a great story to be recapped on a future show.

Combining sly innuendo with the ever present threat that a new couple might actually *have sex* on their weekend away, the show became an instant hit. The Channel Ten news got a stronger lead in, all involved got a pay rise, everyone's a winner, as Hot Chocolate once sang.

As you'd imagine, the real stories happened on the fabled "weekends away". Each trip combined two couples and a Grundy TV staff member there to both "chaperone" the contestants and make sure the film crew got enough to edit a good story on their return.

The show ran for a number of years, and some of the "behind the scenes" tales have become legendary.

Once, a girl decided to swim home to Sydney. From Fiji.

Fortunately she was picked up by a local fisherman about 3km from shore.

When the panic stricken chaperone rang the girl's parents, her mum simply said, *"Oh, you know she must have forgotten to take her meds."*

Suffice to say, that recap never went to air.

When the Perfect Match production moved to Melbourne, many members of the Grundy staff put their hands up to become chaperones. After all, a free weekend in Queensland is always a nice perk. Stupidly, I too put my hand up, and ended up accompanying four bogans (two matched couples) to Surfers' Paradise. As we drove into town from Gold Coast airport, I remember one of the girls say, *"When I was 14, I ran away from home with me boyfriend, and we spent three nights in that bus shelter over there."*

As it turned out, neither of the couples got on in any meaningful away, and the lame footage of them dancing at a dodgy Cavill Avenue nightclub never made it to air. When I got home I told the Executive Producer, *"Never again."*

In its latter incarnation, Perfect Match tried to spice things up a bit by casting older contestants, and for a while it wasn't unusual to see people in their sixties and seventies trying to find their ideal date.

Of course this is not without its obvious risks.

In the late eighties, a 64-year-old woman from Melbourne picked a 73-year-old man as her Perfect Match, and the couple were hastily dispatched to Adelaide to enjoy a weekend together.

At 2am on their first night away, the Perfect Match Executive Producer received a phone call from – let's call her Beryl.

"Hello….what's happening, Beryl? It's 2am…"

"It's Barry. He's died".

"He's died?!! Jesus, have you called the police?"

"No, I'm calling you. I've got two nights left in Adelaide, can you send me another man please?"

True story.

Needless to say, this was hushed up at the time, and TV viewers never discovered what actually happened When Beryl And Barry Went to Adelaide.

Legend has it that Dexter, the talkingPerfect Match robot delivered the eulogy at Barry's funeral.

And as for *Dexter,* the talking Perfect Match robot whose matchmaking one liners were scripted by an underpaid copywriter, he now resides in the Australian Centre for the Moving Image museum in Federation Square, Melbourne.

To this day, the slightly shabby plastic robot is one of the museum's more popular exhibits.

Is the phrase *"Battle of the Sexes"* even relevant today?

Divorces: the divorce rate (divorces per 1,000 marriages) hasn't altered much since 1980, but the number of actual divorces has increased markedly. Roughly, in 1980 40% of marriages ended in divorce. In 2021 it was very close to 50%. As comedian Bill Burr says, *"If they gave you those odds when you went parachuting, you wouldn't fucking jump!"*

The divorce rate rose sharply during the 1970s, mainly due to the introduction of the Commonwealth *Family Law Act* 1975 which made divorces far easier to obtain than the more buttoned-down fifties and sixties.

It would seem a fairly cut-and-dried statistic, but experts seem to disagree on the trends for divorce. Some say it rises each year; others claim it's been on a downward trend since the early 80's. These days it seems that the only people who seem to enjoy a good divorce are the *lawyers.*

Then there is the relatively recent explosion of *online dating.*

Just look at the numbers. Tinder, the undisputed market leader when it comes to online dating, has had over 57 billion, yes that's right, *billion* searches since its inception over a decade ago. This year alone it has 75 million active users worldwide. That's a lot of folks "lookin' fer lerv".

Now whether you swipe left, swipe right, hook up, chat or even quietly move over to your Netflix app, it's a huge number of people trying to meet other people at any one given time.

The gender breakdown is about what you'd expect...77% male and 23% female.

This is about as surprising as seeing a headline in the paper that says, *"Couple Dies After Eating Puffer Fish".*

THE HOLLYWOOD CASTING COUCH

Long synonymous with Old Hollywood, the phrase *"The Casting Couch"* has regained mileage in recent years due to the #metoo movement and publicity surrounding disgraced and convicted movie mogul Harvey Weinstein.

"Sleeping your way to the top" was an unkind but almost recognized way for young actresses to get ahead in showbiz. Or as comedian Kathy Griffin once said, *"I slept my way to the middle."*

In reality, it was just a nasty reflection on the power dynamic between women and the men who hired them.

Veteran Hollywood actor Michael Caine said in 2018,

"We were all aware that the casting couch existed. It was almost a joke. I thought it was terribly unfair that a talented actress might not get a part because she wouldn't do something sexual with the producer. But it happened, and there was nothing I could do about it."

Three time Oscar winner Meryl Streep spoke out about the Harvey Weinstein scandal, telling the Huffington Post that Weinstein's behaviour was *"disgraceful and inexcusable"*, while also saying, *"Not everybody knew"*.

Streep went on to say, *"Harvey was exasperating but respectful with me in our working relationship, but I didn't know about his having meetings in his hotel room or bathroom, or of any inappropriate or coercive acts."*

Actress Glenn Close, who was been nominated for an Academy Award eight times, also went on the record about Weinstein.

Close said, *"I have been aware of rumours that Harvey Weinstein had a pattern of behaving inappropriately around women. He has always been decent to me, but now that the rumours are proving to be true, I feel angry and sad.*

I am angry that the casting couch phenomenon is still a reality in our business; the horrible pressure, the awful expectation put on a woman when a powerful, egotistical, entitled bully expects sexual favours in exchange for a job".

Harvey Weinstein was fired from his job at the company that bore his name, and is currently serving a twenty-three year jail sentence for rape and sexual assault.

Another rumour is that Harvey's penis itself is so ugly that no cosmetic surgery or photoshop wizardry could plausibly turn it into an object any woman would possibly exchange for a movie role.

If you needed proof that the casting couch phenomenon was a long term part of the Hollywood culture, next time you're in Los Angeles pay a visit to the Highland Shopping Centre near Grauman's famous Chinese Theatre.

On a second floor balcony sits an art installation featuring a sculpted fibreglass day bed named – wait for it – "*The Road To Hollywood.*"

The work of Californian artist Erika Rothernberg, the sculpture includes a mosaic "red carpet" and a series of quotes from those who made it into the movie business.

The artist herself does not regard the piece as a casting couch per se, but does hope that visitors will sit on it and take a selfie with the iconic "Hollywood" sign in the background.

There is currently a petition circulating throughout LA to have the sculpture permanently removed.

BILL COSBY

Whenever anyone is accused of sexual assault or rape, they are of course entitled to the presumption of innocence until evidence says otherwise.

But when the accusations start numbering in the dozens or more, even the most capable and confident defence lawyer would surely be tempted to switch off his phone.

Enter "America's Dad", Bill Cosby.

Famous since the 1960's when he became one of the first African-American men to headline comedy clubs and co-star in a national TV show (*"I Spy"* in which he starred opposite Robert Culp), the once much loved Dr. Cliff Huxtable has been accused of various sexual offences a staggering sixty plus times across many states of the union.

When lawyers get involved, time and costs invariably blow out, and in Cosby's case, the statute of limitations in many states meant that numerous cases could not be tried.

After numerous legal shenanigans and career destroying levels of publicity, Cosby was finally sentenced in 2018 to "three to ten years in state prison" for drugging and sexually assaulting Andrea Costand at his home fourteen years earlier.

In June 2021, the Pennsylvania Supreme Court overruled this conviction on technical grounds and Cosby was released from prison.

So, Bonobo Bill? Given the astounding number of complaints about his behaviour, it would be easy to link Bill Cosby with the bonobo gene. But as those little chimps like to say, "There are some things even a bonobo won't do…"

While one simply can't assume Cosby's guilt in every case, the old phrase "Where there's smoke etc." comes to mind. In this case (or sixty cases), that smoke would be enough in Hollywood parlance, to have been a “Towering Inferno”.

Arrogantly assuming this overturned conviction automatically made him “innocent” of all accusations, Cosby then announced he would go back on the road as a stand up comedian.

For those shows (if they ever happen), it would be safe to assume tickets won’t be hard to get.

SIZE MATTERS

According to archaeologists, despite it contradicting what we've already learnt about Adam and Eve, men first came out of the trees some 4.3 million years ago, although some Australian sporting officials might regard that date as a tad premature.

As these early bipeds actually learnt to put one foot in front of the other and walk upon solid earth, their first argument was reputedly over who had the biggest dick.

This primitive "mine's bigger that yours" dispute was the precursor to millions of senseless and irrelevant future debates that all lead to the one inane question:

Does size matter?

When it comes to getting into trouble because of their dicks, movie and screen actors have never been far from the action. Perhaps not always as arrogant or stupid as some sports stars, politicians or Harvey Weinstein.

Nonetheless, many a Hollywood heart-throb have found themselves having to explain their actions, or at the very least, have their *agent* offer a plausible *mea culpa*.

As an actor, your job is basically to "pretend to be someone else". Ego and publicity are part and parcel of the game. And when so much information is spread through rumour and gibberish (I'm looking at you, *publicists)*, interesting facts can sometimes get buried in the noise.

In the showbiz world, a netherland of "prepared statements" and half baked hashtags, some of the greatest rumors of all time have involved actors and the *"size of their dicks"*.

Of course no accurate records exist for this most dubious of stats, so these things are done purely on hearsay and gossip. One Hollywood star, whose reputation has stood the test of time, is the late *Mr Television* himself, Milton Berle.

Legend has it that when he was born, Uncle Miltie's appendage was so impressive, the doctor issued him a "girth certificate".

The late, great American comedian Gilbert Gottfried once wished that Milton Berle was still alive so he could reveal his schlong on Gilbert's incredibly popular podcast. *"It would be like Van Gogh unveiling a new painting"*, he said.

Comic Jeffrey Ross said about Berle's penis, *"I once saw him use it to sink a four foot putt."*

Many a Hollywood contemporary would challenge Milton to a "size contest", and legend has it he would *"only take out enough to win."*

Other movie and TV stars reputedly blessed by the "size fairy" include Liam Neeson, Rodney Dangerfield (*"His balls hung down like a grandfather clock")*, John Hamm, Willem Dafoe and Orlando Bloom.

Other allegedly well endowed celebrities include comedian Bill Hader, "Saturday Night Live" star Pete Davidson, Jared Leto, and David "Bend it like" Beckham.

GLOBAL SHRINKAGE

Earlier we asked the question, "Does Size Matter?"

Of course it depends who you ask really, but what if I was to tell you that according to several scientists, men's penises around the world are *getting smaller* due to our shabby and polluted environment?

American environmental scientist Dr. Shanna Swan from the Icahn School of Medicine at Mt Sinai says that this is an "existential crisis facing humanity".

That's a strong claim.

I prefer to simply call it *"Global Shrinkage"*.

Dr Swan believes this phenomenon is contributing to declining fertility rates, and is due to the presence of phthalates, commonly found in manufactured plastics, and environmental pesticides..

Phthalate Esters impact human genitals by altering the hormone-producing endocrine system, and consequently leading to more baby boys born with smaller penises.

Dr Swan based her findings on research involving rats, where exposure to phthalates increased the likelihood of the rat being born with shrunken genitals.

The actual chemical originates from some plastics, baby toys and foods, and works by mimicking the hormone oestrogen and disrupting the natural production of hormones in humans, later affecting sexual and genital development in children.

In an earlier study published by Dr Swan in 2017, it was found that sperm levels have dropped by more than half over the past forty years.

At this rate, Swan believes that most men will be unable to produce viable sperm by 2045.

Now for every yin there has to be a yang. And you guessed it, another study actually says men's penises are getting larger rather than smaller.

Who do we believe?

Recent research from the *World Journal of Mens Health* states that the average penis size has grown 24% over the past thirty years.

So what have we really got here – global shrinkage or global engorgement?

Let's be honest; for most blokes, a 24% size increase would be barely noticeable to the naked eye. Though many would argue it's still far better than the alternative.

The research was conducted at Stanford University in California, and they suggested that this ongoing penile inflation was a result of pollution, junk food, and sedentary lifestyle. The good news about this of course, is that if you want a larger member, all you need to do is live next to an Indian cricket ground, sit around all day and order in KFC.

One thinks it's probably not that simple.

The study's author, Dr. Michael Eisenberg said, "Any overall change in development is concerning, as our reproductive system is one of the most important parts of human biology. If we're seeing this fast of a change, it means something powerful is happening to our bodies."

Given that he was expecting a result similar to Dr. Swan's, where penis length was *declining*, the Stanford guru simply says, "More research is necessary".

So does the average bloke care whether there's a scientifically proven, generational, statistical change in the size of his dick, or, as I would argue, "size" is generally in the eye of the beholder.

As far as the bonobo is concerned, there are reportedly only about two thousand of these sex-crazed mini chimps left in the wild, and as discussed earlier, what the bonobo may lack in size, is certainly made up for in enthusiasm and bad behaviour.

WHEN THINGS GO WRONG

My first "real" job was at a rock n roll radio station in Melbourne. Actually it was the number one station in the city, and renowned around Australia for its high ratings and cooler than hell DJ's. What is the collective noun for DJ's? A *turntable* of DJ's? A *joint?*

Who knows? But at 1422 3XY it's wasn't unusual to see record company mogul Michael Gudinski cruising and schmoozing the halls while trying to get airplay for his latest album or signing. Or as I spotted in the boardroom one Friday night, Brian May from *Queen,* who were currently touring the country. Brian seemed a nice enough bloke for a world famous rock god, and possibly the only world famous rock god to also have a Ph.D in astrophysics.

One week it was rumoured that the great man himself, Paul McCartney was going to visit the radio station, but as it turned out, it was just a surly member of his backing band, *Wings.* No rock god there, just an ego in a pair of denim overalls that made him look like the bloke who resets the pins in a bowling alley.

When you combine "rock radio station" with the 1980's, it's no surprise that the joint was a hotbed of illicit sex and soft drugs. Only one of the much vaunted "jocks" was married, and was thus regarded with a mixture of pity and suspicion.

I became very good mates with one of the stations's sales reps. The sales guys all dressed like Don Johnson in *"Miami Vice",* and strutted round the place selling sponsorships to nightclubs and car yards. One of the most popular sponsorships was with a hot new Car Sound Emporium. Yeah, it actually called itself an "emporium".

It was popular with the staff because you could get a 40% discount on new car cassette decks. CD's, and FM radio had not yet reared their heads.

MP3 and streaming was decades away.

My mate the sales rep (names withheld to protect the guilty) had been having an on again, off again fling with a girl from the programming department. Her job was to basically type up memos and running sheets, and keep the boardroom fridge full of beer, just in case, you know, James Reyne or Jimmy Barnes popped in.

Trouble was, the girl from programming wanted to keep this fling "quiet", and my loudmouthed mate seems to have more listeners than the breakfast show. Everyone at the station had heard all the gory details about this "quiet" fling.

She knew he'd been mouthing off about their relationship all over the radio station, so in bed that night, instead of "inhaling" during a certain sex act, she bit down. Hard.

As he said afterward, *"like a chimp chewing through a two inch jungle vine".*

He may have been kidding himself about the "two inch thick vine", but there was no doubt she did some serious damage to his dick. His foreskin, while not necessarily "shredded", certainly had a new hole or two in it, and doctors quickly decided to perform an operation that would normally have been done shortly after his birth some twenty-five years previous.

Pain from the stitches meant he couldn't wear any more tight-fitting suit pants, so for the next month, he swanned about the radio station wearing loose tracksuit pants and a blue bathrobe, looking like a blonde tipped Hugh Hefner.

While it would be unfair (and slightly distasteful) to say he *"milked"* the situation, it certainly raised his popularity with the female staff members who were more than keen to get a look at "his stiches". And being a sales rep, he was happy to show them the prospectus.

As for his now ex-girlfriend from the programming department, she was immediately nicknamed "Jaws", a nom de plume she seemed more than happy with.

ARE MEN NECESSARY?

When asked if the world really needed men, legendary Australian feminist and academic Germaine Greer said,

"A society can survive with only one man, but no society will survive a shortage of women. If you are fool enough to produce 40 million sperm with each ejaculation, you'd have to be aware that all but one or two of you are surplus to requirements."

With a strike rate lower than a Bangla Desh opening batsman, why do we bother? That's a helluva lot of unused sperm. Every single time.

Not that I've ever heard one man say, *"Well that was a waste..."*

So are men useful? In what ways? The *breadwinner?* Maybe a hundred years ago, but not relevant today.

Odd jobs around the house?

Hunting vermin? Washing the car?

As George Carlin once said: *"Woman are crazy, and men are stupid. And woman are crazy because men are stupid."*

There's been plenty of recent talk that men may be on their way out genetically anyway.

In fact, some recent research has suggested that the Y sex chromosome, which only men carry, may become extinct in as little as five million years time, or before St Kilda win their next premiership.

In 2003, genetics professor Brian Sykes predicted the end of the Y chromosome, and by extension, *men,* would become extinct in less than 100,000 years.

But Jennifer Hughes and fellow scientists at the Whitehead Institute in Cambridge, Massachusetts declare that rumours of the Y chromosome's demise have been greatly exaggerated. Compared with that of the chimpanzee, whose lineage diverged from that of humans about six million years ago, Ms Hughes stated, *"The Y chromosome is not going anywhere, and gene loss has probably come to a halt."*

"I'm not saying it won't happen, but for the next 25 million years or so, I'm extremely confident the penis is here to stay".

OK, I completely made up that last statement, but you can see what she's getting at.

THE TEFLON DICK

We all know that one guy who, in matters of love and flesh, seems to get away with murder.

Not literally of course, otherwise he'd be spending the next couple of decades sharing an exercise yard with Tony Mokbel.

But figuratively, here's a guy who is never held to account for his questionable behaviour, and appears to slide effortlessly from one relationship to the next.

He's like a bonobo but with the gift of the gab.

He has what is known as, a *Teflon Dick.* Nothing ever sticks.

You know the bloke. Not only can he sleep with his girlfriend's *best friend*, but somehow still remain on speaking terms with them both.

He can even sleep with his *best mate's* girlfriend, but he'll generally get away with this one, since his best mate will blame the girlfriend, not him.

I never said this was fair, it's just an observation.

Then there's the guy who has a constant string of stunning girlfriends, and still manages to stay best buddies with all of them.

This latter type is sometimes known as a *Leonardo,* named after Hollywood A-Lister, DiCaprio.

The Oscar-winning actor has long been renowned and admired for his seemingly endless parade of girlfriends, all of whom tick three main boxes.

1. Under 25 years old.
2. Stunningly attractive.
3. Happy to be traded.

While hosting the 2020 Golden Globes, Ricky Gervais mentioned the actor's latest movie, *"Once Upon A Time In Hollywood"*;

"The film is nearly three hours long. By the end, Leo's date was too old for him".

Most of his girlfriends have been actresses or models, and the roll call has been impressive, to say the least.

Since his breakthrough films *"Romeo & Juliet"*, and *"Titanic"*, DiCaprio's string of lovers has included the following names:

Bridget Hall; Brittany Daniel; Naomi Campbell; Kristen Zang; Helena Christensen; Amber Valletta; Bijou Phillips; Eva Herzegova; Gisele Bundchen; Bar Rafaelli; Anna Vyalitsyna; Blake Lively; Erin Heatherton; Toni Garnn; Rihanna; Kelly Rohrbach; Laura Whitmore; Nina Agdal; Georgia Fowler; Juliette Perkins; Camila Morrone; and Maria Beregova.

To his great credit, none of Leo's paramours seemed to have ever had a bad word to say about him, which suggests either he's a fantastic bloke and lover, or his lawyers have crafted a near flawless "Non Disclosure Agreement".

One doesn't have to be a movie star of course to enjoy a full polyamorous existence. Although to be fair, it helps.

According to his biography, prior to marrying Annette Benning, legendary Lothario Warren Beatty had reportedly bedded 12,575 women. Surely he'd forgotten a few, so I'd suggest if we rounded up the figure to around 13,000 we'd probably have a more accurate tally.

I used to work with a bloke whose girlfriend once caught him in *their own bed* with another girl.

Now the phrase in flagrante delicto may sound like something that is served with a cherry in a cocktail glass, but it merely means being caught *"on the job"*, as it were.

"On the job" is exactly how the long departed newspaper *"The Truth"* described circumstances surrounding the death of former politician and attorney general, Sir Billy Snedden. According to the coroner's report, Snedden died of a heart attack, which the *Truth* maintained occurred while the former Liberal leader was having sex with his son's ex-girlfriend. Sordid, sure, but when the final result is *death* you could hardly accuse him of "getting away with it".

This work mate of mine, who was already regarded as one of the world's great bullshitters, managed to convince his girlfriend she was *"dreaming"* that she'd seen him in bed (*her bed)* with another girl. He was that persuasive she ended up apologizing to *him* for even suggesting such a thing. As I say, the true GOAT.

Many other political figures over the ages have enjoyed the notoriety of the *Teflon dick.*

Long –serving Australian Prime Minister Bob Hawke was a legendary "pants man", as was US President John F. Kennedy. And despite the countless conspiracy theories surrounding the Kennedy assassination, nobody has yet suggested that Lee Harvey Oswald pulled the trigger due to a *"love dispute"*.

That's not to say JFK didn't have a touch of the Teflon about him. Back in the sixties, the Secret Service was all about keeping his servicing secret.

In 2022, a Southwest Airlines pilot took to the plane's intercom system while en route to Cabo San Lucas in Mexico, and threatened to return the aircraft to its LAX departure gate if passengers didn't stop sending him nude photos through their iPhones' Air Drop feature.

DICKING ALL OVER THE WORLD

As mentioned earlier, the Bonobo is only found in a small area in the Democratic Republic of Congo, though it's influence (and if you believe my theory, its *genes*) extends right across the entire globe.

So if you ever want to see a large group of grown men dressed in drag and carrying gigantic replicas of penises, forget the Sydney Gay & Lesbian Mardi Gras.

Try Japan instead.

On the first Sunday of every April, the Japanese city of Kawasaki unleashes (or perhaps that should be *unsheathes)* its annual Festival of the Steel Phallus, a tradition that dates back to the seventeenth century.

It's the Kanamara Matsuri, to use its correct name, and every year well over 100,000 people visit this small city south of Tokyo to pay homage to the male member.

Why? Legend holds that a jealous, sharp-toothed demon once hid inside a goddess and bit off the penises of her first two husbands. While the alleged goddess may have been the Lorena Bobbitt of her time, she somehow managed to get married a third time. A brave man to walk down that aisle, one would imagine.

But hubby number three was made of sterner stuff, and being a blacksmith by trade, fashioned himself a penis made of solid cast iron, thus making his member impervious to the sharpened dental work hidden inside his new missus.

Seems a tough way to win over the new bride, but eventually, so the story goes, love managed to conquer all. No mention though on how he coped with the inevitable *rust.*

These days, a visit to the festival will entail thousands of people carrying large papier mache genitals, holding up penis shaped candies, and waving colourful, anime inspired flags.

The whole thing sounds quaint and faintly ridiculous in today's politically correct world, but this Japanese Dick Festival brings in a huge amount of money each year, most of which goes to AIDS research.

Nestled in the Himalayas, the small country of Bhutan is known for its monasteries, fortresses and dramatic landscapes that vary from sub tropical plains to large mountains and valleys.

It's also a popular trekking and hiking destination for westerners, and here's a tip. The country's official language is known as Dzongkhan, and even the locals struggle with it.

Why does it get a mention in this book? Well, Bhutan also has a social fascination with the human penis. It actually has a strong historic and spiritual significance. It's not often that the phallus is linked to religion, but in Bhutan some sections of the population actually worship the penis and see it as a symbol of strength and faith.

Throughout the country, colourful phallic symbols adorn every second building, and while they may surprise or even shock the odd western tourist, are a graphic reminder of Bhutan's religious history.

These colourful dick pics are testament to a 15th century Tibetan saint, or *lama,* by the name of Drupka Kunley. Now old Drupka was seemingly possessed with the Bonobo Gene, and this was made abundantly clear in his philandering behaviour, sexually charged sermons, and a number of born-out-of-wedlock offspring.

Legend has it that he was once gifted with a holy ribbon to wear around his neck, but he instead tied it around his penis, hoping it would bring him "luck with the ladies".

It's no wonder there are huge colourful penises on the walls and houses of Bhutan, and indeed many of them have a "divine ribbon" tied around them.

Seven hundred year old superstition, or evidence of the Bonobo Gene. You be the judge.

And try as I may, I haven't been able to translate the phrase "dick pic" into Dzongkhan.

"She wanted to keep the whole affair quiet, and he apparently had more listeners than the breakfast show."

TIGER WOODS

Tiger Woods has won 82 PGA Tour titles.

Some have unkindly suggested that his tally of extra-marital affairs may have even eclipsed that rarified figure, a record of PGA victories that he shares with the great Sam Snead.

Tiger has also won 15 major titles. And when it comes to "majors", getting caught with your pants down by your wife is some qualification.

Woods was the first athlete to earn $1 billion, though it would be fair to say his ex-wife Elin Nordegren may have claimed a reasonable chunk of his fortune in their divorce settlement.

There were plenty of rumours about Tiger's indiscretions off the golf course, but as so often happens among high achieving, high net worth *men* is that What Happens on the Tour Stays on the Tour.

Until a fateful night in November 2009 when Tiger crashed his car outside his Florida mansion at 2am.

His Cadillac Escalade SUV collided with a fire hydrant, several hedges and a tree. His then wife Elle Nordegrin rescued the unconscious golf legend by smashing a window in the car with – you guessed it – a golf club.

No reports though on whether it was a wood or long iron.

It later emerged that he had been repeatedly cheating on his wife, and they divorced a year later, with Woods reportedly paying her a settlement in excess of $100 million.

In 2017, Tiger was found passed out behind the wheel of his Mercedes, with police discovering a number of prescription drugs in his system. The $250 fine wouldn't have troubled the bank balance too much, but Woods later said he was "seeking professional help to manage his medications".

Tiger Woods's worst road trauma occurred in 2021 when he was involved in a high-speed crash in Palos Verdes, California, near Los Angeles. The 45-year-old superstar was cut from the wreckage of his Genesis GV80 by firefighters after the vehicle had rolled several times.

Woods was rushed to hospital where he was treated for "comminuted fractures" in the upper and lower parts of the tibia and fibula, meaning the breaks had led to bone splintering.

The LA County Sherriff said afterwards that Woods was "lucky to be alive".

He has barely played golf since, and it looks like his record of fifteen Major titles will unfortunately never increase.

For a bloke with near superhuman eye/hand coordination, you'd have to say Tiger Woods was one lousy driver.

Which is a helluva thing to say about the man who was the world's number one golfer for an astounding 281 consecutive weeks.

Bonobo Gene? I'd like to think that with Tiger Woods it was more a combination of hubris, arrogance and extremely deep pockets.

WILT "THE STILT" CHAMBERLAIN

Already 6'11" (210cm) by the time he started high school, Philadelphia-born Wilt Chamberlain was always too busy smashing records on the athletics track to bother with basketball, which he then regarded as a *"game for sissies"*.

But since "basketball was king in Philly", young Wilt soon found himself the starting centre in the Overbrook High School team.

Described as *"out and out frightening"* due to his size, strength and athleticism, it was then he was first christened "The Stilt", a nickname he would drive all the way to the NBA.

After dominating his first two college seasons, he wanted to try his luck in the big time, but NBA rules at the time stipulated that teams could only draft players who had completed their college education. So instead he joined the famous Harlem Globetrotters on a $50,000 annual contract, a slab of money that these days would equate to a yearly salary of nearly half a million dollars.

But big Wilt didn't just make hay. He also liked a roll in it. Liked it very much. So much that he claims to have slept with more than 20,000 women over his career.

Now, do the maths here. Assuming this elite level satyriasis didn't kick in until he'd begun his fifteen year professional career, that's about three different women *every single day* after turning pro. This is a strike rate that can only be described as *"Jaggeresque"*. And as we know, despite the double negative in his song lyric, one thing Mick *was* able to get was Satisfaction.

And even if we amortise the 20,000 figure across his entire forty-five year adult life, it was still *more than one woman* every single day.

He was one fully committed athlete. And one thing the never married basketballer was committed to was surely his *"lack of commitment"* when it came to women.

Chamberlain was always extremely popular with teammates, opponents and fans, and it was not an uncommon sight to see the 7'2" superstar strolling through the streets of Philadelphia, happily acknowledging the tooting car horns of passing motorists and the swarms of adoring kids that would follow him along the footpath.

There is one curious statistic however. After his alleged twenty thousand casual sexual encounters, not once did he claim to have fathered a single child. Although in recent years, a San Francisco man by the name of Aaron Levi claimed to be the illegitimate son of the great Wilt Chamberlain. Levi, now around sixty years old, says he was the result of a two day fling between the basketball star and his mother while playing in California.

Levi's mother has always maintained that Wilt was the father, but Chamberlain himself never acknowledged the story, and even today, surviving members of Chamberlain's family refuse to allow a DNA test to prove the claim either way.

GENE SIMMONS

Egotism and self-importance are common traits in show business, but few embody them so completely as 73-year-old Chaim Witz, better known as the driving force behind KISS, *Gene Simmons*. His arrogance and ego are legendary, and not without some justification.

With a net worth of between $400 and $500 million, he is one of the richest rock stars on the planet, and this is due to a business acumen that has seen him license the KISS brand across more than 3,000 products from clothing to condoms, credit cards to caskets, action figures to guitars.

The KISS brand itself is valued at close to 1 billion dollars.

But of course, nobody gets a spot in this book for simply being a rich bastard.

I'm just surprised they never came out with a licensed KISS Bonobo plush toy. Surely a sex-crazed miniature chimp with a sequined guitar round its neck would have sold millions.

Prior to his (still going) thirty year-marriage to former Playboy playmate Shannon Tweed, Gene Simmons did what rock stars have been doing since Litle Richard first sang "A Wop Bop A loo Bop, A lop Boom Pow". And that of course was to sleep with as many women as possible.

Though maybe Little Richard didn't sleep with that many *women,* if you get my drift.

A drug and alcohol teetotaller (itself a rarity in rock n roll), The KISS Demon claims to have slept with more than 4,800 women in his single days.

"I have bedded nearly 5,000 groupies", said Simmons.

"But my wife made me burn all the Polaroids".

That must have been a helluva bonfire of the vanities.

Some of Gene Simmons many girlfriends over the years included:

Liv Ullman, Katey *"Married With Children"* Sagal, Cher and Diana Ross.

Simmons' "partner in crime" has always been singer and guitarist Paul Stanley, who also is one of the richest men in rock. The other original members of KISS – drummer Peter Criss and guitarist Ace Frehley both succumbed to the usual rock n roll temptations along the way and were fired by Simmons and Stanley in 1980 and 1982 respectively.

Various other musicians have joined the band and performed with them over the years, but true KISS fans always preferred the original line up, and both Peter Criss and Ace Frehley have returned to tour with the band on a number of occasions since being first being fired. One imagines this has been more of a business than musical decision from Gene Simmons and Paul Stanley.

Currently in the middle of their *third* and supposedly final "Farewell Tour", both Gene and Paul have expressed a desire for the two original members to participate in the very last show. Gene Simmons doubts though whether this will happen.

Ace Frehley's major vice appears to have been alcohol and its effect on let's say, his *reliability.*

In 1997 I was lucky enough to witness this first hand.

As part of the "Alive/Reunion" Tour with all four original members, the band played three nights at Melbourne's Rod Laver Arena.

While working on the Eric Bana Show, we arranged for Eric to meet the band in their dressing room before they went on stage. Eric was done up as one of his more popular characters – the mulleted, semi-literate bogan *"Poida"*.

To my great amazement (why didn't I take a *camera?!)*

I found myself in KISS's dressing rooms just as they were putting the finishing touches to their make up. Assuming they would have an army of make up artists, I was pleasantly surprised to see that all four band members still applied their own stage make up before every show.

Apart from Gene Simmons, Paul Stanley, Ace Frehley and Peter Criss, the dressing room contained a couple of stage managers, Eric as "Poida", director Jon Olb, myself, plus a cameraman and sound recordist.

"Poida" recorded a quick interview with the band before they grabbed their guitars and prepared to hit the stage.

All business as usual, Gene shook our hands and said, *"Got what you needed? OK, let's go and rock...."*

And this was when I realized Ace Frehley was perhaps not as switched on as the other band members.

"This way, gents", said a stagehand, leading them out the door. Once in the corridor, Gene, Paul and Peter turned left up the stairs to where you could hear the anticipatory hum of 12,000 rabid Kiss fans.

Ace Frehley turned right and wandered aimlessly down a darkened hallway.

"Ace has gone the wrong way", I laughed.

"Jesus", said Jon to our cameraman. *"Did you get that?"*

"This way, Ace" said Eric as Poida.

Meanwhile, Gene Simmons, his frustration clearly visible beneath his thick black and white "Demon" make up, looked like he was about to belt Ace across the head with his bass.

As we giggled like idiots we then heard the legendary opening voice over for KISS's live show...

"You wanted the best. You got the best. The hottest band in the world... KISS!"

Smoke, flames, flashing strobes, screaming crowd....the pure adrenalin rush of a rock n roll show.

You couldn't help yourself. By the end of the gig, all of us were punching the air and singing *"I wanna rock n roll all nite and party every day!"*

"In the sixties, the Secret Service was all about keeping the servicing secret."

MALCOLM, WHERE'S YOUR TROUSERS?

In late1975, Australia was in the midst of a full blown constitutional crisis, when the opposition Liberal party, led by Malcolm Fraser, blocked supply to the senate, controlled by the Labor government, which was led by inconoclastic Prime Minister, Gough Whitlam.

On November 11, Whitlam visited the Attorney General, Sir John Kerr to request a double dissolution of both houses of parliament, this bringing on a federal election.

Instead, Kerr sacked him on the spot, and Fraser became the Australian PM.

Fraser was your classic Tory conservative, a wealthy grazier from Victoria's western district, whose jutting jaw and unsmiling countenance made him rich fodder for political cartoonists, who often depicted him as an "Easter Island statue".

Fraser won the ensuing election in a landslide and remained PM until being defeated in 1983 by the charismatic Bob Hawke. His tenure as PM was fairly stable, and it was only after losing that election that Malcolm Fraser became a much more intriguing figure.

Three years after losing office, the former PM was in the American city of Memphis, Tennessee where he was to give a speech at a local country club.

After the gig, he took a cab to the famous Beale Street music district. (Who knew that the granite faced ex-PM was a closet blues man?) He was intending to have a drink at the luxurious Peabody Hotel, but somehow ended up at the far less salubrious Admiral Benbow Inn sometime after midnight, where he checked in as *"John Jones from Victoria".* He is also said to have paid the tariff with an aggressively waved $100 bill.

The next morning Fraser appeared in the hotel lobby wrapped in a small towel, complaining he had lost his $10,000 Rolex watch, passport, wallet, a handful of cash, and as was plain for the receptionist to see, his *trousers.*

At 193cm (6'4"), Malcolm's trousers were in their own right, a substantial piece of material, and the fact that he had "misplaced" them caused great mirth in not only the hotel lobby, but also back in his home country of Australia.

Fraser told a local newspaper he didn't report the robbery as he had a *"busy schedule to keep and the chances of getting my stuff back seemed pretty remote".*

He also believed his drink had been drugged. Most locals thought he had been rolled by one of Beale Street's many "ladies of the night", most of whom had never before met a former world leader.

A Memphis taxi driver gave Fraser a pair of his own trousers to wear, and moaned later that he'd never got them back. *"They was good pants too"*, he said.

While proving great fodder for Australia's satirists and cartoonists, the truth about Malcolm Fraser's night in America's blues capital has remained a curious mystery to this day.

"I wish I'd never gone to bloody Memphis", he said afterwards.

SIMPLY RED – WELL, THE TIP IS

Why is it when some male braggart boasts about how many women he's slept with, he always rounds the number up to the nearest hundred?

Once you're at that level, surely you've lost count?

Mick Hucknall, lead singer of 80's band *Simply Red,* not only possesses a voice like smooth molasses and a shock of red curly hair, but also claims to have bedded 1,300 women at the height of his fame.

He said, "I was single, touring the world and being a playboy. I didn't really know what I was doing."

One could argue he knew *exactly* what he was doing, and doing it pretty well.

His list of conquests included actresses, models, other musicians, and even sports stars. Money wasn't "too tight to mention" as he worked his way through an A-list of lovers, including Catherine Zeta-Jones, Helena Cristensen, Lady Victoria Harvey, and the winner of 22 major tennis titles, German ace Steffi Graf.

"You're only here once", Hucknall explained. "It's good to have all the experiences one can have". And as he went on to confirm that sometimes he bedded three different women a day, it could be said he was never guilty of *"Holding Back The Years"*.

Hucknall was once described in the British press as "pop's greatest Lothario", a title he surely could have shared with dozens of others.

It should be noted here that the word *"Lothario"* derives from the old French word *Lothaire,* literally meaning "famous warrior".

It's at this point we should acknowledge another renowned womanizer from ancient history (not that the 1980's is all that *ancient).*

I speak of course of the legendary King Solomon, wealthy monarch of the Jewish Kingdom whose reign ran from 970-931 BC. Solomon was reputed to possess wisdom personally granted by God. During his forty years on the throne, countless people would travel great distances to seek his advice.

As wise a counsel he may have been to strangers, his own life was far more complex. He is said to have married 700 women *(700!)*, and often boasted of his love of money and riches. Seems he would have needed a healthy bank account to pay for 700 divorces.

This is where the phrase *The Solomon Paradox* derives from. It's a phenomenon where we have wiser advice for others than we take upon ourselves.

Rather than Mick Hucknall's life on the carnal rock n roll highway, Solomon's *"do as I say, not as I do"* doctrine is clearly the blueprint for countless modern day politicians and business leaders.

Though these men may have lived around 3,000 years apart, their bonobo-like behaviour is still worthy of scrutiny and ridicule.

Being a King or a redhead is still a poor excuse for being a dickhead.

GROUPIES

Always somewhat looked down upon, groupies were girls who hung around bands (especially back in the 60's/70s).

Sex was invariably involved, but always consensual. These days, they would be known as *"stalkers"*, and would possibly run into intervention and protection orders.

Though in Cameron Crowe's brilliant 2000 film *"Almost Famous"*, actress Kate Hudson, playing groupie Penny Lane, utters the film's most poignant line, when she says,

"We don't have intercourse with them. We inspire the music. We're here because of the music."

Probably the most famous of all the so called "groupies" was Pamela Des Barres who documented her life in her very readable memoir, *"I'm With The Band: Confessions of a Groupie"*.

Set in the late sixties/early seventies when rock 'n' roll was just becoming mainstream, Des Barres blows the lid off the sex & drugs lifestyle behind the scenes. It's not all she blows.

She also claims to have knocked back a "date" with Elvis Presley.

For the record, she *didn't* knock back dates with Mick Jagger, Jimmy Page, Keith Moon, Waylon Jennings, Chris Hillman, Noel Redding, Gram Parsons, Don Johnson and Jim Morrison.

One of the most famous groupies of all time was Cynthia Albritton, better known as *Cynthia Plaster Caster.*

A visual artist, her claim to fame was making plaster casts of rock stars' erect penises. Her first and most famous "client' was guitarist Jimi Hendrix.

"It was exciting just catching the elevator up to his hotel room. Usually I had to climb up the fire escape."

Her clever and accurate notion that once cast, the penis would go flaccid and be easily removed from the cast greatly amused rock guitarist and bandleader Frank Zappa who became one of her great supporters, though he was never interested in being part of the plastering process himself.

Her list of cast members included the great Eric Burdon of the Animals, Noel Redding from Hendrix's band; Wayne Kramer from the MC5, actor and songwriter Anthony Newley (*"What Kind of Fool Am I?"*, and punk rocker Jello Biafra.

Spare a thought for Buzzcocks singer Pete Shelley who submitted to the process, but whose cast was never finished, due to "mold failure".

In 2000, Cynthia held her first exhibition in New York of all her casts, and she has been the subject of several documentaries quite a few songs.

So were there male groupies who followed around the female stars?

If you believe the legend, Janis Joplin had and satisfied a countless procession of male suitors/groupies.

But according to the women themselves, most of the action seemed to go the other way. As Susanna Hoffs from The Bangles said, *"We used to bring the cute guys back stage to chat and flirt. But that was as far as it went."*

Neko Case, once voted by Playboy readers as the "sexiest woman in Indie rock" said, *"Ladies in bands don't get ANY action. None. Back me up on this, girls."*

So why don't female rock stars get groupies?

Many men don't like the reversed power dynamic of going "cap in hand" to the woman they idolize and then be judged through the same prism of attractiveness that female groupies have to face. To wit; a lot of men simply don't know how to approach or handle a powerful woman.

One female rock star simply said, *"Backstage we are surrounded by DUDES 100% of the time. Bunch of cock blockers!"*

The worst theory I have read about why women don't get male groupies is this:

Men find it harder to get through security.

FUN FACT

The Beatles' *"She Came In Through the Bathroom Window"* was written after a bunch of girls broke into Paul McCartney's house.

THE ERECTION INDUSTRY

In 1989, a group of pharmaceutical chemists were working in a research facility in Sandwich, England owned by chemical behemoth, *Pfizer.*

While trying to find a drug used to treat hypertension (high blood pressure) and angina pectoris (a symptom of ischaemic heart disease) they managed to synthesize a compound named Sildenafil citrate. Early clinical trials were conducted in Morriston Hospital in Swansea. These first trials suggested the compound had very little effect on angina, but did induce marked penile erections.

Bingo. You can imagine the meeting at Pfizer right after the testing process…

"So Trev, how's our potential new blood pressure drug coming along? You done the testing?"

"Yeah…well..um….."

"So how effective is it? Hypertension down 30%, right? "

"Well, it's just that….'

"Spit it out, man! How soon can we get it to market?"

"It doesn't work."

"What do you mean it doesn't work?"

"It doesn't reduce your blood pressure. It doesn't cure your angina. But!"

"But what?"

"It's a big but, boss.."

"Speak to me, son".

"It makes your penis hard for up to eight hours at a time."

"Say that again…"

You can almost see the cash registers spinning behind his eyes.

"There are a few minor side effects though".

"Side effects??! Mate if a bloke hasn't had a boner for six months, he could grow moose antlers out of his forehead and he'd still buy the stuff..."

Pfizer immediately saw the potential of the drug and decided to market it there and then as a panacea for erectile disfunction.

The word Viagra is I believe, Latin for *"licence to print money"*.

"This is better than curing cancer", one senior Pfizer exec was heard to say at the time.

Viagra went on sale in 1998, and in its first two months its sales exceeded $182 million, which was twice the combined income of the five next most successful drug launches. Viagra sales hit $1 billion in its very first year, and have hovered around that mark ever since.

Despite several competitors now in the market, Viagra still maintains its position as the number one cure for erectile disfunction.

The following is a true story.

One of Australia's leading "celebrity chefs", you know, TV, radio, magazine columns, cookbooks etc told me this story at a corporate golf day.

He (who must remain nameless) and his wife had two terrific kids, and decided to go for a third. Despite months of trying, his wife failed to get pregnant, and she laid the blame squarely at her hubby's feet.

"There's nothing wrong with me. You go and get yourself checked out!"

So off he went to the Men's Fertility Clinic at Melbourne's St Vincent's Hospital.

As he filled out the various forms on arrival, the young female receptionist handed him a smallish glass jar.

"Of course, we're going to need a sample", she said.

"If you could just pop into that room and give us a sample, that would be great. No rush though, in your own time."

As he said to me, *"I thought that in circumstances such as this, they provided some, you know, reading material of a certain type, to help facilitate the process.*

But not a thing. The room was bare."

Using a combination of muscle memory and imagination, our dexterous TV cook managed to eventually provide said sample. *"Not easy to catch it in the jar though..."*

He then returned to reception and handed the jar to the young, attractive nurse. She looked at it, turned it over in her hands, then looked at it again before speaking up.

Urine sample, Mr. -----, we were after a URINE sample".

Given he was a television chef, it's lucky he didn't say, "Well here's one we prepared earlier..."

"Viagra is a Latin word, meaning 'licence to print money'.

THINKING OF BUYING A CONVERTIBLE?

British scientists believe they have established a link between penis size and the desire to own a sports car.

Investigating whether there is "any truth to the cliché that a man driving an expensive sports car is somehow compensating for his male inadequacy", a team from the Department of Experimental Psychology at the University College in London surveyed 200 men between the ages of 18 and 74.

They claim to have established *"a casual psychological link between fast cars and small penises for the first time."*

The study found that men, particularly those aged over 30 "rated sports cars as more desirable when they were made to feel they had a small penis."

The team behind the survey told some participants that the average penis size was 18 centimetres (7 inches), while others were told it was 10 centimetres (4 inches).

Men who were misled by the former claim were more likely to desire a sports car.

The trial manipulated self-esteem in different ways and measured ratings for other luxury products, but found no connection between anatomy and the desire to own objects.

Scientists at the London College believe *"the luxury automotive industry may be unwilling to acknowledge this link"*.

MALE NUDITY ON TV

It wasn't that long ago that the only way you'd see a male appendage on television would be if you'd managed to reconnect your ancient VHS machine after finding a milk crate of old pornos in the back shed.

And despite your blurry, third generation dub of the Pamela Anderson/Tommy Lee tape, back in the day, penises simply weren't seen on the telly. These days on the other hand, seeing a dick on the TV is like seeing a tennis ball during Wimbledon.

2022 was truly a banner year for full frontal male nudity.

It's a little reminiscent of when cable TV first hit our screens. Because you *paid for it,* and thus wasn't free-to-air (FTA), cable was a lot more relaxed as far as nudity, violence and swearing. The difference these days is *streaming.* It's a lot like cable, only you can watch your programmes *when you want to.*

The Netflix series *Minx* is set during the 1970's porn blitz in California, specifically a nude magazine aimed at a female audience.

Minx actually showed more than 100 penises in its first season alone. And over on HBO they weren't too shabby either, with its drama *Euphoria* revealing thirty in one episode.

As *Minx* show runner Ellen Rapaport said: *"Avoiding full frontal men would be like showing somebody who runs a restaurant but not showing the kitchen."*

One upside to the penis proliferation on our televisions these days is that it has created a new series of jobs in the production business.

These jobs are for *Intimacy Co-ordinators.* While there doesn't seem to be any hard and fast rules for what an Intimacy Co-ordinator actually does, reports from Hollywood seem to indicate the job is primarily to reassure actors (both male and female) that the on screen nudity is not only crucial to the production's storyline but will be filmed in a way that is acceptable to all involved. At least nobody is going with the old cliché of trying to justify the nudity as being *"tasteful"*.

While there's little doubt the Intimacy Co-ordinator is an important role these days, personally I'd prefer it if they just renamed the position as *"Wang Wrangler"*.

Twice Oscar-nominated actor Mark Wahlberg played an up and coming porn star in Paul Thomas Anderson's 1997 epic *"Boogie Nights"*, and finally revealed his footlong schlong at the end of the film, bringing a collective gasp to the movie audience.

Unfortunately the penis was a specially made prosthetic, but the good news is Wahlberg hung onto the prop after the film was completed and now keeps it in a safe at his home.

I keep it in the safe", said Wahlberg, *"in case one of my kids is rummaging around looking for a phone charger or something and stumble upon it. What's this, dad?"*

As far as movie memorabilia goes, it may not be up there with the original *Maltese Falcon,* but Dirk Diggler's diggler would surely fetch a decent sum should it ever go under the auctioneer's hammer.

A RANDOM SELECTION OF MALE STUPIDITY

"The problem with the world is that fools and fanatics are always so sure of themselves, and wise people so full of doubts."
– Bertrand Russell

The Real Thing?

Recent studies in China have revealed that men who drink large amounts of Coca-Cola and/or Pepsi, can lead to larger testicles and higher testosterone levels.

The Northwestern Minzu University in China was trying to determine the impact of carbonated drinks on fertility and sex organs in men.

The study looked at three groups of mice – it's always *mice* – one that only drank water, and two that drank Coke and Pepsi for fifteen days.

The study concluded that "drinking Coke and Pepsi could promote testicular development and enhance testosterone secretion."

This survey does though contradict previous studies that showed that those men who drank a litre of Coke a day had 30% less sperm than those who didn't drink it at all.

As far as I know, there have been no studies to see what happens to the size of your testes if you drop a Mentos into the Coke before consuming.

That's not a brush, THIS is a brush...

Canadian Brent Ray Fraser is a performance artist and former erotic model whose unique talents were unearthed on the TV franchise *"France's Got Talent"*.

He whipped out his todger and used it to paint a detailed portrait of the show's judges. That's right, a Penis Painter who with a lick of acrylic and a swirl of his member can create something that will brighten any wall of your house. Of course, the finished painting has to be "well hung".

Sure beats finger painting.

Rather not go to court over this....

A Norwegian company invented some ultra-soft underwear and ran into trouble with the United States Patent & Trademark office when it tried to register the brand name *"Comfyballs."*

Their request was denied on the grounds that the *"U.S. public would find the name vulgar"*.

Back to the drawing board, the company faced no opposition when they renamed the product *"iNuts"*.

Vanity Fair

When it comes to plastic surgery, especially that for "vanity" reasons, most people naturally assume that women are the most likely to "have work done".

But according to the American Society of Plastic Surgery, over 80% of procedures each year are carried out on *"men"*.

And some of those procedures are the most delicate of all – *"penis augmentation"*.

Now there is the "easy" version of this procedure, and the "difficult" version. The first involves the injection of "dermal filler" to make the thing appear larger, and the second, and most complicated involves cutting the thin skin of the penis and inserting solid enhancements underneath.

This doesn't just augment the penis; it also greatly increases the risk of infection, which if you remember Malcolm Macdonald from Chapter 3, involves the very real risk of it – quote – *"dropping off"*.

And nobody needs a phone call from their surgeon saying, *"You know that augmentation procedure we did? It went horribly, horribly wrong"*.

Art is in the Eye of the Beholder

YESS Electrical, a British wholesaler of electrical products, conducted a survey for some reason as to what people were most likely to draw with their finger on a dirt-covered white van.

Apparenly, the vast majority of men would draw a "dick and balls", while the majority of women would write *"Clean Me"*.

Not Today, Folks.

While researching this book, I came across (sorry), an article titled "*9 Places Never To Stick Your Penis.*"

If you need to look up this article, you are an idiot, and please go on to the next chapter.

Now that's a compliment

Another true story. During the 1980s, a good looking young man earned his living by not only playing top level Australian Rules football, but also regularly appeared as a male model on a top rating TV game show.

His chiselled good looks combined with the allure of the professional sportsman made him something of a household name in his native city of Melbourne.

A couple of years into his football career, he sustained a nasty injury to his right knee, one that required surgery to fix.

The local showbiz media treated the story with the same breathless enthusiasm as it would open heart surgery to the Prime Minister. *Would he ever play again? Would he lose his good looks?*

Countless column inches were devoted to the injury and the likelihood of his complete recovery. For a humble medial ligament, one almost expected candlelit vigils and a telethon to pay the young man's medical bills.

As his gurney was wheeled down the corridors toward the operating theatre, a gaggle of nurses watched as if the leader of the free world was about to undergo life threatening open heart surgery.

Of course, his knee was cleaned up and a couple of hours later he was wheeled into the recovery room. Still a little groggy from the anaesthetic, he lifted the bedsheet to check out his knee, only to see a perfectly formed pink silk ribbon tied around the base of his penis.

When I asked him which of the nurses he thought may have been responsible, he simply grinned and said, "All of them…."

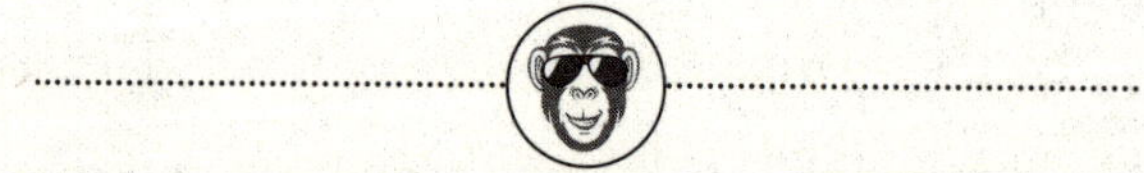

"That's not a butt call, this is a butt call."

A good mate of mine from Sydney's northern beaches – let's call him *"Whitey"* – is one of those common middle-aged golfers. He plays 2-3 times a week and his game never improves.

This is despite the countless thousands of dollars he has spent on the latest, professionally endorsed and recommended equipment.

One of his most cherished pieces of golf gear is – was – his electric golf buggy. It magically transports his clubs around the course at the touch of a button. After all, why spoil a good game of golf by actually *carrying your clubs?*

During a recent game he had played his drive up the eighteenth hole, and pondering his approach shot into the green. Once he'd decided on his next club, he looked around for his buggy, which should have been 10-15 metres away.

There was no sign of it.

Dashing to the side of the fairway, he was just able to see the tip of his driver slowly sinking into a beautifully manicured lake.

He'd been carrying the remote control in his back pocket and realized he'd inadvertently pushed the button a few times with his arse, sending the electric cart across the fairway like a Taylor Made Transformer, slinking into a cold and watery grave.

By the time he got to the edge of the lake, his playing partners were offering him plenty of advice, as in *"It's OK, I'm videoing the whole thing"*.

Stripping off his golf gear, Whitey plunged into the eel-filled icy depths. It wasn't just his clubs and buggy he wanted back; in the bag was his mobile phone, wallet and expensive range finder.

After much effort, he managed to retrieve the whole thing, although as he said recently, *"the fucking phone hasn't worked properly since."*

Cap? Gone. Spare glove? Gone. Range Finder? Gone. Wallet? Soaked. New box of Titleists? Gone.

His playing partner immediately posted the video to the club's website, and even included a few still shots for posterity and the "laugh factor".

As it turned out, the video footage was a crucial piece of evidence when he tried to claim the wrecked moto-buggy on his insurance.

His insurance assessor even asked if he could keep the video as a *"learning tool"* for his staff.

The Golf Club Captain also put forward a motion at the annual general meeting to name the sloping piece of fairway that helped claim the buggy as *"Whitey Hill"*.

He now has new clubs, a new buggy, a new phone, and his game still has not improved one iota.

The Darwin Awards

Named after the father of the evolution theory, the Darwin Awards commemorate those who improve the gene pool by removing themselves from it in the stupidest way possible.

The theory being that their actions ensures the long term survival of the species, by selectively allowing one less idiot to survive.

And here's a surprise, since the Darwin Awards began in 1985, nearly 90% of the winners have been men.

Let's raise our glasses to the 2022 winner….a Russian soldier – let's call him *Yuri* - on duty in the invasion of Ukraine found an abandoned Apple Macbook. Now a Moscow-purchased Macbook would have put something of a dent in his weekly Russian army pay check, so Yuri decided to swipe it. To be fair, he wasn't the first and won't be the last soldier to loot something from a battlefield.

But where to hide it?

He quickly slid the slim computer into his chest armor pocket, replacing a solid ballistic armor plate that was designed to save his life.

Unfortunately for Yuri, while on patrol in the town of Irkin, a Ukraine bullet ended both his life and new Macbook.

One of my favourites occurred in Brazil in 2006, when a man decided to disassemble a Rocket Propelled Grenade (RPG) by driving back and forth over it in his car. This technique didn't work so he took to bashing it with a sledgehammer. Second time lucky, kind of. The ensuing explosion killed not only our man, but also destroyed six cars and the workshop.

This is the great thing about the Darwin Awards – they are all awarded *posthumously.*

Ah... footballers...

Former AFL star Scott Cummings played for four different clubs – Essendon, Port Adelaide, West Coast Eagles and Collingwood - and kicked 349 goals across his 128 games.

To use his full and correct title, *1999 Coleman Medallist Scott Cummings* has since built a steady career behind the microphone as a radio host and football commentator.

Playing for four clubs gave Cummings an enormous number of former teammates to call upon when asked to contribute a "dumb bloke" story for this book.

"I won't name this fella", he says, *"but he was never the sharpest tool in the shed, especially when covering his tracks."*

Apparently Scotty's teammate had been living with his girlfriend for a number of years when, as he says, *"had one on the side"*.

Now he wasn't the first, and he won't be the last sportsman to cheat on his partner, and he may well have got away with it, until he was returning home from an interstate football match only to be met at the airport by not only his girlfriend but also *"the one on the side"*.

Not only was he now single again, but the tribunal deemed his behavior as *"reckless and high impact"*.

Basketball legend and online gambling spruiker Shaquille O'Neal was once asked if he visited the Parthenon after a recent trip to Greece.

Shaq's reply? *"I can't really remember the names of the nightclubs we went to..."*

"It wasn't me, Officer..."

Police in the Colorado town of Springfield recently pulled over a driver after they clocked him doing 52mph in a 30 zone.

As the cops approached the car, the driver put his dog in the driver's seat, and moved himself into the passenger seat.

"I wasn't driving, officer", the man is reported to have said.

The police report suggested that the driver was intoxicated at the time.

He was consequently booked for drunk driving, speeding and resisting arrest.

It should be pointed out that this was not the town of Springfield from *"The Simpsons"*.

The dog was let off with a warning.

A couple of generations ago, tattoos were generally only seen on bikies, criminals, returned soldiers, and the occasional "trying to look tough" rock star.

Today they are common in all parts of society; in fact in the USA, over 40% of millennials have at least one tattoo on their body.

The inherent potential problem of injecting permanent ink beneath one's skin has not changed though over the years. And that problem is, *what if I change my mind?*

Any red blooded American can see a business opportunity when it arises, and thus, one of the country's hottest growing cottage industries these days is, of course...tattoo removal. Getting rid of this unwanted in-skin artwork is worth more than $30 million a year and is growing at an exponential rate.

Naturally, most of the customers are men, and in more than 95% of cases, the tattoo they want removed is, wait for it....*a girl's name.*

"Walk a bit faster, son"

As described earlier in this book, when it comes to Dumb Behavior, footballers of every code seem to vie for superiority. In 1992, the Adelaide Crows, a professional club in the Australian Football League conducted a pre-season training camp and bonding exercise.

A team building expert from Canberra briefed the players on the exercise to which they were about to commit. Their task on this day was to walk, bare feet, across red hot coals. This was to test the *"power of their mind"*.

Adelaide young gun Nigel Smart was first cab off the rank.

Assisted by two teammates, he quickly set off across the fire pit, the coals glowing at close to 1000 degrees centigrade.

In an outcome that would have surprised few, he suffered third degree burns to the soles of his feet and did not play football again until Round 7 of the 1992 season.

As Smart said afterwards, *"that's when I got the nickname Notso..."*

More Stupid Celebrities

Whether it's due to the fame factor, wealth or simply the *"nobody ever says no to them"*, celebrities often feel they can behave any way they like with impunity.

Arrogance and ego can only carry you so far, so it's fair to say we all enjoy the hubris around celebs behaving stupidly.

Among recent examples of Dumb Celebrity Behaviour, the first award must go to box office juggernaut and *(so we thought)* all round nice guy Will Smith.

The *"Aladdin"* and *"Men In Black"* star earnt his place here after his performance at the 2022 Oscars.

When host Chris Rock made a joke about Smith's wife suffering the balding disease alopecia, the former rapper strode from his seat onto the stage and slapped Rock across the face.

Now in very few workplaces is it acceptable to physically assault someone, and Will Smith, with one well-timed round arm right hand, did not do himself or his wife Jada Pinkett Smith any favours.

And let's be honest; Smith had a 10cm height and 20kg weight advantage over the 178cm comedian. In boxing terms, Rock was well out of his weight division.

While some like to look at Smith's actions as *"defending his wife's honour"*, it was a pretty dumb thing to do, especially since Rock's only crime was to make a pretty lame joke. And what would the Oscars be without some pretty lame jokes? Just ask the great David Letterman, who openly admits he *"bombed"* when he hosted the 1995 telecast.

Perhaps Will Smith was smarting because of the poor box office returns from some of his most recent films. I mean, there hasn't been a $900 million *"Independence Day"* or $1 billion *"Aladdin"* for a while.

Still, this being Hollywood, not more than thirty minutes after clocking Chris Rock, the Academy awarded Will Smith the "Best Actor" Oscar for his portrayal of "King Richard" Williams, father of tennis stars Venus and Serena.

He'll still have to just watch it on TV for the next decade after copping a ten year ban on attending the event by the Academy of Motion Picture Arts and Sciences.

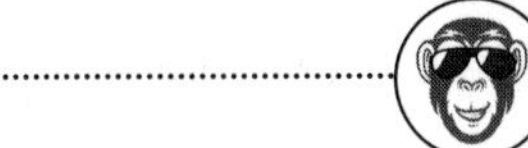

THE FINAL CHAPTER

So after all that, is it the male's fault? Are men always that dumb?

Or is it, as I have suggested, a ridiculous genetic mishmash that human men somehow share with a sex crazed, vertically challenged primate from a small patch of darkest Africa? A moronic mélange that is barely even visible under a scientist's microscope.

Seems like a bit of a stretch, I'll admit.

But is it really? It's true that in this book we have barely scratched the surface when it comes to examples of Stupid Male Behaviour.

I mean, if you thought that the 824 pages of Dostoyevsky's *"The Brothers Karamazov"* was a long read, wait until you get to the yet-to-be-written *Encyclopedia of Idiot Footballers (All Codes).*

If there's been something of an ongoing focus in this book, it has been a gratuitous (and possibly *unhealthy)* emphasis on the male member itself.

But can we blame a single piece of anatomy? It seems a lot of responsibility to be heaped on one small tube of skin and blood vessels.

I've stated before that my Bonobo Gene theory is just that – a theory. Now let's look at it – the Bonobo is a sex crazed, small primate that is prone to violence, and also has the ability to walk upright. Sound like anyone you know?

And if we do share 98.7% DNA, who is to say that some of our more "behaviour challenged' men haven't been born with 99% or 99.5% Bonobo DNA?

Bear that in mind next time you hear about a bloke urinating on the front door of a house, and then taking out his key to go in.

After all, it's just a theory. And theories can only be proved or disproved when tested and studied by qualified scientists.

With blinding optimism, I am already planning a sequel to this humble book.

"The Bonobo Gene 2" will hopefully be rolling off the presses sometime in early 2024.

And this is where you, the reader, comes in.

Just about everyone, male, female or something in between, has a story about Stupid Male Behaviour.

And I want to hear them.

Just tales, preferably tall and true. I don't think we'll need photographs.

Simply go to: ***www.thebonobogene.com***

Email me at ***steve@thebonobogene.com***

Hit me up on instagram: ***@thebonobogene***

Hope you enjoyed this book and I look forward to hearing from you.

Steve Marshall